T0330015

Creating Value through Innovation

To Simonetta and Tommaso

Creating Value through Innovation

Angelo Dringoli

Faculty of Economics, University of Siena, Italy

Edward Elgar

Cheltenham, UK • Northampton, MA, USA

Published by
Edward Elgar Publishing Limited
The Lypiatts
15 Lansdown Road
Cheltenham
Glos GL50 2JA
UK

Edward Elgar Publishing, Inc.
William Pratt House
9 Dewey Court
Northampton
Massachusetts 01060
USA

A catalogue record for this book
is available from the British Library

Library of Congress Control Number: 2009922769

ISBN 978 1 84844 329 7

Printed and bound by MPG Books Group, UK

Contents

Abbreviations

t	Period of time (year)
T	Process or product lifetime (years)
S	Period up to the structural change (years)
N	Period up to a terminal date
$FCFO(t)$	Free cash flow from operations in period t
$V(0)$	Firm value at initial date 0
$D(0)$	Value of debt
$E(0)$	Value of equity
TV	Terminal value of the firm
$P(t)$	Product price in period t
$C(t)$	Current operating cost of product
$Q_V(t)$	Quantity of product sold
$Q_P(t)$	Quantity of product produced
$Q(t)$	Quantity of product produced and sold
K_M	Technical coefficient of raw material
K_L	Technical coefficient of direct labour
K_E	Technical coefficient of energy
$EBITDA(t)$	Earnings before interest, taxes and depreciation
$m(t)$	Unit margin
$A(t)$	Depreciation and amortization
$WC(t)$	Working capital (difference between current assets and current liabilities)
ΔWC	Change in net working capital
$I(t)$	Capital expenditures (plant and machinery)
$I_{R\&D}(t)$	Investment in R&D
$I_{MK}(t)$	Investment in marketing activities
ρ	Weighted average cost of capital ($WACC$)
g	Growth rate
τ	Corporate tax rate
τ^*	Adjusted corporate tax rate

r	Rate of deterioration of technical structure
s	Expected inflation rate
λ	Rate of increase of labour productivity
φ	Rate of reduction of product sales
γ	Rate of price reduction due to product innovations
δ	Rate of price reduction due to process innovations

Preface

Maintaining competitive advantage once gained is not easy for firms operating in industries characterized by rapid technical progress, significant changes in consumers' behaviour and tastes and strong competition among firms. It is worth remembering the cases of many successful firms with strong market positions which collapsed within only a few years or were taken over and reshaped.

To avoid strategy myopia, the management has to concentrate on the sustainability of value in the long term, especially in a highly competitive environment, such as that which characterizes many sectors of the world economy today.

Managing the firm in highly competitive markets means systematically researching new competitive advantages, not defending those previously acquired. The most effective way to surprise competitors and create new competitive advantage is to innovate products and processes.

To continue creating value entrepreneurs must look towards the future, design the change of the firm's structure and systematically organize the production of innovations. They have to identify the fundamental trends which are progressively eroding the competitive advantage of the firm and create the innovation strategy which is necessary for rebuilding competitive advantage and new value.

This study emphasizes this strategy as an instrument for building new competitive advantages, not for defending the existing ones. The proposed model focuses on the sustainability of firm value, the implementation of product and process innovation strategies, to be realized with the intensity and the frequency required by the dynamic competition in the industry.

The innovation strategies take on a central relevance for the sustainability of firm value. Without a good strategy it is not possible to obtain a positive cash flow, in the long run, in industries characterized by rapid technical progress and where the firms are highly competitive.

In this book we propose some quantitative models to be used for determining the value of the innovation strategies in highly dynamic and competitive industries. They point out the economic variables and relations on which the value of strategy depends and the conditions for creating a sustainable value. The analysis also aims at identifying the resources and competences the firm has to develop as well as the organizational structure needed for carrying out such innovative processes.

According to this approach, the most relevant contribution of the management consists precisely in the vision of business evolution, the identification of the necessary innovation strategies and the implementation of the structural changes of the firm.

The book develops a rationalist, analytical approach to strategic management, following what has become termed the 'design school' of strategy. The approach, linking strategy to finance and organization, is normative, as it aims to help managers to develop value-enhancing strategies, promoting sound, relevant and applicable analysis. The conceptual framework is followed by analytical models and simulation to offer useful frames to guide decisions.

We believe that the structural or activities-based view of the firm can be an effective framework for the aim of this study, especially for reliably assessing the economic value of strategies. However, we widely use the resource-based view of the firm and the dynamic capabilities framework for useful insights concerning the sustainability of value.

The analysis is specific to highly competitive industries and it principally refers to medium and large industrial firms.

In Chapter 1 the firm value is presented as the result of firm structure, environment trends and strategies, emphasizing the temporality element of competitive advantage in highly competitive industries. In Chapter 2, the principal determinants of operating cash flows are examined: firm structure, competitive positioning and the environment changes. In Chapter 3 the fundamental innovation strategies are defined with reference to the main changing forces of industries.

In Chapter 4 the strategy used for creating value by process innovation is examined. A quantitative model is proposed for determining the value of productivity improvement strategy. Similarly, in Chapter 5 the product innovation strategy is examined and a quantitative model is presented for determining the economic value of this strategy. In both cases simulations are conducted so as to ascertain the sensibility of the models with respect to the various parameters and variables.

In Chapter 6 integrated strategies of product and process innovations are evaluated, using a more complex quantitative model. In Chapter 7 the organizational structures for continuing with the innovative processes are analysed, particularly the internal R&D venturing, the strategic alliances and outsourcing. Finally, Chapter 8 summarizes the conditions for sustainability of value in firms operating in highly innovative environments.

In order to increase the value of this book for readers, some examples and cases are included in Strategic Focus sections, presented at the end of

Chapters 2–7. They make the concepts in each chapter come alive for the reader and facilitate learning, showing the utility of concepts and quantitative models previously presented and therefore provide a link between the theory and application.

This book has been designed for advanced students of strategic management and finance. We also believe it can be useful for managers interested in the issues and topics of investment and strategy.

Prof. Angelo Dringoli
Siena, September 2008

1. The value of the firm in highly competitive industries

INTRODUCTION AND OBJECTIVES

The value of a firm is based on its current and predicted operating cash flows. The first depends on the firm's existing structure and its competitive positioning; the second depends on the trends in the environment and the new configuration of the firm, that is the strategy accomplished by the entrepreneur to cope with the new competitive forces.

Strategy is seen as a decision to change the firm's structure. Therefore, adopting a strategy means choosing which structural change to adopt and how to reconfigure the firm's system to maintain its value.

In sectors with high innovation rates, cash flows show high variability in relation to the environment dynamics and the success of development strategies. In these conditions it is necessary to identify the strategy to pursue for rebuilding the competitive advantage and creating new value. With this aim an analytical model is set up for evaluating the economic conditions under which an innovation strategy creates value.

THE VALUE OF THE FIRM: THE GENERAL MODEL

Corporate finance literature has emphasized that the value of the firm is obtained by discounting expected free cash flows from operations $FCFO(t)$, realized in the business lifetime, at the weighted average cost of capital ρ (Copeland and Weston 1988; Brealey and Myers 1996; Ross, Westerfield and Jaffe 1999).

In the case of an unlimited lifetime period, the value of the firm $V(0)$ can be calculated as follows:

$$V(0) = \sum_{t=1}^{\infty} \frac{FCFO(t)}{(1+\rho)^t} \tag{1.1}$$

with free cash flows from operations in period t (year), $FCFO(t)$, equal to cash flows from operations $CFO(t)$ minus working capital change $\Delta WC(t)$ and the capital expenditures $I(t)$ necessary for maintaining the efficiency of the firm and favouring its growth; the weighted average cost of capital ρ is the cost of the different components of financing used by the firm, weighted by their market value proportions ($WACC$).

The standard approach for determining this value requires to estimate the operating cash flows for a future period S, for example 3 or 5 years (short-term cash flows), and then to estimate the cash flows for the following periods (long-term cash flows).

If the cash flows in the last period S remain constant for an unlimited period of time (long-term cash flows), we will have:

$$V(0) = \sum_{t=1}^{S} \frac{FCFO(t)}{(1+\rho)^t} + \frac{FCFO(S+1)}{\rho} \frac{1}{(1+\rho)^S} \tag{1.2}$$

If the cash flows in the last period S grow at a constant rate g for an unlimited period of time, corresponding to the growth rate of the economy or of the industry, we will have:

$$V(0) = \sum_{t=1}^{S} \frac{FCFO(t)}{(1+\rho)^t} + \frac{FCFO(S+1)}{(\rho-g)} \frac{1}{(1+\rho)^S} \tag{1.3}$$

This is the standard model widely used in theory and in practice for evaluating firms.

The general formula for estimating the cost of capital ($WACC$) is as follows:

$$WACC = \rho = kd\frac{D}{V} + ke\frac{E}{V} \tag{1.4}$$

where kd is the cost of debt and ke the cost of equity, D the value of debt and E the value of equity.

The equity value E is equal to the difference between the value of the firm, as the whole of activities V, and the value of financial debts D:

$$E(0) = V(0) - D(0) \tag{1.5}$$

The following description shows the determinants of free cash flows from operations $FCFO$ in period t:

+	Revenues	R
−	Current operating expenses	C
=	Earnings before interest, taxes and depreciation	EBITDA
−	Depreciation and amortization	A
=	Earnings before interest and taxes	EBIT
−	Interest expenses	INT
=	Taxable income	EBT
−	Taxes	EBT tc
=	Net income	NI
+	Interest expenses	INT
=	Net operating profit after taxes	NOPAT
+	Depreciation and amortization	A
=	Cash flow from operations	CFO
−	Working capital change	ΔWC
−	Capital expenditures	I
=	Free cash flow from operations	FCFO

where: tc is the tax rate on net income (corporate profit). That is:

$$FCFO = (EBITDA - A - INT)(1 - tc) + INT + A - \Delta WC - I \qquad (1.6)$$

$$= EBITDA(1 - tc) + A\,tc + INT\,tc - \Delta WC - I \qquad (1.7)$$

Note that in the leveraged firm the *FCFO* is increased by the tax benefit (*INT tc*) deriving from the application of corporate tax to earnings after interest.

THE VALUE OF THE FIRM AS A FUNCTION OF MANAGERIAL ECONOMIC VARIABLES

In order to determine the value of the firm, we prefer to disregard the financial tax benefits, rightly reducing the cost of debt by tax rate, $k_d(1 - tc)$, in the expression of weighted average cost of capital (*WACC*), as the majority of financial literature does.[1] That is:

$$FCFO(t) = EBITDA(t)(1 - tc) + A(t)\,tc - \Delta WC - I(t) \qquad (1.8)$$

$$WACC = \rho = kd\,(1-tc)\frac{D}{V} + ke\frac{E}{V} \qquad (1.9)$$

The *WACC* depends on the cost of funds, *kd* (debt), *ke* (equity) and the capital structure of the firm (*D/V* and *E/V*).

The *EBITDA(t)* depends on the quantities of product sold $Q_v(t)$, the sale price *P(t)* and the current operating expenses *C(t)*.

We will express *EBITDA(t)* as:

$$EBITDA(t) = [P(t)-C(t)]\,Q(t) \qquad (1.10)$$

To simplify the analysis, we will also consider the tax benefits from depreciation through an appropriate reduction of the tax rate on *EBITDA* (with $\tau^* < tc$). The expression (1.8) becomes:

$$FCFO(t) = EBITDA(t)\,(1-\tau^*)\ -\Delta WC(t)\ -\ I\,(t)$$

$$= [P(t)-C\,(t)]\,Q(t)\,(1-\tau^*)-\Delta WC(t)-I\,(t) \qquad (1.11)$$

Considering the difficulty in estimating the relevant variables precisely, this expedient may be accepted for an analysis aimed at ascertaining the conditions for a profitable strategy, in terms which cannot be reduced to a marginal analysis.[2]

This solution is very useful, because it enables the representation of the *FCFO* and consequently of the firm value, as a function of the most relevant economic variables of the business management. These are the variables under the evaluation and control of the management: product prices, unit costs, quantities and investments.[3]

Note that in the absence of changes in the working capital (that is zero sales growth), the *FCFO* equals the *EBITDA* after taxes, minus the current investment *I(t)*, necessary to maintain the programmed *EBITDA*:

$$FCFO\,(t) = EBITDA\,(1-\tau^*) - I(t)$$

$$= [P(t)-C(t)]\,Q(t)\,(1-\tau^*)-I(t) \qquad (1.12)$$

Figure 1.1 shows the determinants of value: benefits provided by the product, unit margin, costs and volume (*Q* = number of units sold) (Ghemawat 1991). Margins (*P* − *C*) depend basically on the differential benefits provided to consumers. Volumes (*Q*) depend on the organization size and costs which in turn reflect on price. Costs to the organization and benefits (the advantages which products may provide to consumers compared with those of competitors) determine the unit margin, that is the difference between price and cost. However, benefits and costs also influence the production volumes and consequently the total margin.

Within the industry, the firm may create value in many different ways in relation to the importance given to each of the four value determinants: product benefits, organization costs, unit margin and sale volumes. Each strategy tends to leverage on one of these factors (Porter 1980).

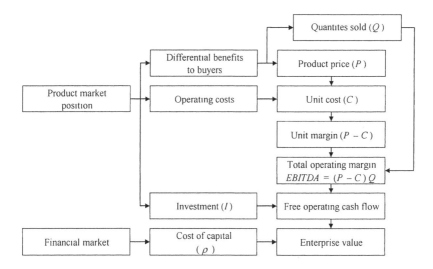

Figure 1.1   Framework for the analysis of value

COMPETITIVE ADVANTAGE AND CASH FLOW DYNAMICS

In industries characterized by high environment dynamics and hyper competition, the competitive advantage of a successful firm is continuously eroded by rival firms and operating earnings (*EBITDA*) tend to decline rapidly.[4] Competitive advantages are temporary, because of the rapid technical progress and the change in consumers' preferences and behaviour.

In this kind of business even surviving is difficult. The innovation of industrial processes and products reduces the margins and sales of firms operating with out-of-date structures.

Examples of successful enterprises that have quickly fallen into deep crisis have been numerous over the last decades. Furthermore, very few firms that were leaders in the 1980s were in the same position at the end of the decade. IBM, Texas Instruments, Xerox, Digital Equipment (DEC), Du Pont, PanAm, TWA and many others experienced the rapid erosion of their competitive advantage, because of the significant technological changes introduced by incumbents and non-traditional competitors (Hamel and Prahalad 1994).

Innovation is usually induced by a technical progress which cannot be simply incorporated in the existing structure of the firm through incremental interventions. Thus, the firm structure has to be largely re-projected, radically modified and re-constituted at certain intervals of time (discrete intervals), in order to create new positive operating earnings and cash flows.

In general, these structural changes cannot be realized through a continuous flow of 'maintenance' investment $I(t)$, but they require relevant investments concentrated in time. This happens, for example, when new production technologies, enabled by scientific and technical progress, require the building of new plant to be fully exploited or the radical transformation of the existing structures. In other cases there are new products, enabled by technical progress and responding to new consumers' preferences, which require new production and marketing systems.

The automobile, pharmaceutical, micro-processor and other industries provide emblematic examples of the conditions mentioned above. In other words, the change of the firm's structure does not represent an ordinary managerial activity. It is the result of a strategy, which implies process and product innovations, with relevant investments, producing a discontinuity in firm life.

Considering all that, it is necessary to take into account different dynamics of operating earnings and cash flows and use a different analytical model for determining the firm value. These are the outlines of the model we propose.

1. Once a new structure has been established and a competitive advantage achieved, at the beginning the firm will gain high operating cash flows, but these will tend to decrease in time to zero and then to negative values (Figure 1.2). This is due to the progressive erosion of the initial competitive advantage and the growing efficiency gap of the present structure (plant and products) with respect to innovations introduced soon after by competitors.
2. Before the operating cash flow becomes negative, it will be necessary to modify the structure of the firm again, introducing new products or processes. In fact, the decreasing pattern of operating cash flows will be modified only by a new change to the firm structure, with investment in new plant and products. This will happen after a period of time, the length of which principally depends on the environment dynamics and the pressure from competitors.

3. Only after the new structure of the firm is established and innovation is successful will operating cash flows again assume positive values; however they will decrease, after a certain period of time, due to the effects of new competition (Figure 1.2).
4. The dynamics of firm cash flows show a strong discontinuity because the innovation adopted by the management, in order to recover the competitive advantage, has been progressively reduced and then cancelled by the competitive forces.[5]
5. Without innovations and structural changes it is not possible to maintain positive cash flows in the long run and the terminal value of the firm will tend to zero or to the liquidation value of assets.

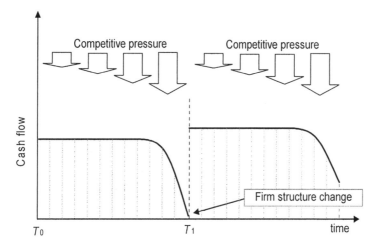

Note: $T_0, T_1 \ldots$ indicate the time of structural changes of the firm.

Figure 1.2   Operating cash flow dynamics of a successful firm in highly competitive industries

INNOVATION STRATEGIES AND SUSTAINABLE VALUE IN HIGHLY COMPETITIVE INDUSTRIES: A NEW ANALYTICAL MODEL OF FIRM VALUE

According to our approach, for creating value it is necessary to:

1. exploit the competitive advantage with relation to the existing firm structure and the competitive positioning;

2. identify the competitive forces eroding the value of the firm;
3. define and carry out the structural changes required by the environmental dynamics.

Exploiting the existing structure is necessary for extracting all positive cash flows from investments already made. Moreover, each transformation of the firm's structure has to be followed by a period of time in which the characteristics of the structure are stabilized and turned into standards; instrumental devices, procedures and organizational criteria remain constant *pro tempore*, representing the stable components of the firm's lifetime. This tuning process, following a development phase, represents the stabilization process of the firm.

Continuously transforming the firm is strongly prevented by the fact that equipment, machinery, and technical devices are firm-specific and not easily negotiable on the market. Therefore, the differences between buying and selling prices are not proportional to the period of time the structure persists and to the production quantities obtained.

Usually the longer the period of time the structure persists with the repetition of the same processes using the existing apparatus, and the larger the cumulative production, the lower the fixed costs are per unit product. Obviously, investments devoted to the establishment of organizational capabilities (sales force, relationships with suppliers, competencies and know-how) are more specific than investments in fixed capital (plant, buildings, and devices) and thus more difficult to sell. Consider, for example, the know-how gained by the firm through R&D activities for making a new product not launched on the market.

Also learning processes represent rigidity factors, because they require time to be fully exploited. Newness of methods, devices and organizational structures prevents the workers from having the competence necessary for achieving new efficiency levels immediately. These will be achieved only through the repetition of operations and the standardization of products, methods and control procedures.

Thus, once the structural change is achieved, the management must aim at the highest exploitation of opportunities in relation to the existing structure of the firm. This implies a systematic activity directed at the standardization of behavioural models and at maximizing the efficiency levels.

But, with time, the firm will be increasingly exposed to the aggressive action of innovations by competitors and environmental changes. The operating cash flow will decrease more and more rapidly, until it reaches negative values as the consequence of the erosion of the competitive advantage. The re-equilibrium action made by the top management will be increasingly difficult; in the end it will be necessary to accomplish a further change to the firm's structure (structural development), so as to create a new competitive advantage. Obviously, the greater the innovative content of a change, the longer the stabilization process will last (market and technology conditions unchanged).

The definition of the strategy represents the critical moment of the entrepreneurial action aimed at creating value.

The change of the existing structure of the firm is necessary to stop the decrease of operating flows, related to the erosion of the competitive advantage due to the aging of the existing structure. This change is not incremental but it represents a significant 'discontinuity' both for the required amount of financial resources and the extent of changes in the technical and marketing sub-structures of the firm.

In this context, using the standard model for calculating the firm value can provoke serious mistakes. It means, indeed, assuming that a firm will realize constant or increasing cash flows for subsequent unlimited periods, after a first period S, on the basis of a flow of incremental investments $I(t)$.

We believe, on the contrary, that the environment dynamics require an explicit definition of the development strategy and of investments needed for its realization and the appraisal of the consequent cash flows.

With this aim in mind, we propose the following analytical model of the firm value:

$$V(0) = \sum_{t=1}^{S} \frac{EBITDA(t)\,(1-\tau^*)}{(1+\rho)^t} + VSTRAT(S)\,\frac{1}{(1+\rho)^S} + \frac{TV(N)}{(1+\rho)^N} \qquad (1.13)$$

where:

$$VSTRAT(S) = -I(S) + \sum_{t=S}^{N} \frac{EBITDA(t)(1-\tau^*)}{(1+\rho)^t} \qquad (1.14)$$

The first term in expression (1.13) is the value determined by the operating cash flows produced by the existing firm structure and the positioning of the firm against the competing forces of the industry. The $EBITDA(t)$ will tend to decrease in time until $t = S$.

The second term is the value of the innovation strategy, where $I(S)$ is the investment needed for realizing the strategy and ρ is the cost of capital. The $EBITDA(t)$ in period $S+1$, $S+2$,...N, depends on the new firm structure, resulting from the adopted strategy. $TV(N)$ is the terminal value of the firm after the period N, at the end of the effects of the development strategy.

If a new structural change is accomplished at time N, the value of the new strategy has to be valued, and so on for the following times. So, in theory, the determination of the terminal value of the firm would require the consideration of a chain of structural changes and the evaluation of their effects, until the end of the firm's activities.

If no structural change has been planned at the end of period S (or at the end of period N), the operating cash flow will fall to zero and the terminal value $TV(N)$ will be equal to zero or at the most to the liquidation value of assets. In fact, with no structural changes, the net operating flows will decrease to zero and negative values, because of the environmental trends and the progressive erosion of the competitive advantage.

To summarize, we believe it is not realistic to assume, after a certain period S, a constant rate of growth of operating cash flow, as a consequence of a programmed flow of investments, growing at a constant rate for an unlimited period of time. This assumption, even if largely used in financial applications, is very prominent in highly competitive industries, because it implies that the firm would carry out a successful infinite chain of structural changes, that is a successful infinite sequence of innovations.

We want to point out that the definition of the strategy and its evaluation, at least for the interval of time including the first 'renewal' of the existing structure, must be at the core of the CEO's efforts to create a sustainable firm value.

To define a development strategy correctly, we need to analyse the external environment, in order to identify the competitive forces threatening the value creation process and the environment trends changing the competitive conditions of the industry in the long run.

We also need to study inside the firm in order to identify the opportunities coming from its existing structure, that is all the stable relationships characterizing the firm. The structure of the firm is the basis of the learning processes and the accumulation of know-how which take place within the firm. It is the stability of characteristics, processes, relationships and transactions that gives rise to and feeds the speciality functional competences constituting the cultural asset of the firm at the basis of innovations. This knowledge is therefore not easily transferable outside the firm.

In choosing the strategy the entrepreneur will have to exploit the 'culture' of the firm: the accumulation of its exclusive knowledge and lever on its knowledge assets. In this view, the firm will tend to operate within an 'oriented dominion' where it is more capable of facing up to the uncertainty and complexity of the environment, fully and creatively exploiting its own knowledge assets.

The awareness of firm structure is essential for defining the development pattern, so extrapolating the privileged evolutionary trajectories from the existing structure. That means capturing the opportunities provided by the availability of exclusive know-how and developing innovations based on accumulated knowledge and techniques.

In conclusion, net operating cash flows depend on:

1. the present structure of the firm, and therefore the characteristics of products, costs and prices (Dringoli 2000 and 2006);
2. the industry's competitive forces: buyers, existing rival firms and potential entrants, suppliers, substitute products or services (Porter 1980); these are forces influencing the sale prices and volumes, in addition to costs of production factors;
3. the environment/market dynamics which influence prices, volumes and costs of production factors;
4. the projected new structure of the firm and therefore the new prices, operating costs and sale volumes determined by the changes which have been achieved.

The operating cash flows in the short term will depend on the existing structure of the firm and its competitive positioning, while the cash flows expected in the long term will depend on the environmental dynamics and the new firm structure defined by the strategy.

According to this view, there is a 'strong' causal link between the preceding and subsequent structural configurations of a firm, in relation to both the material and the immaterial factors. In other words, the characteristics of the new configuration are founded on the material and immaterial resources belonging to the existing structure. Most of them are specific know-how related to the internal and external processes of the firm, accumulated information in the production and sales processes, etc. In fact, in its intangible part, the structure of the firm is essentially a 'container of memory', which expresses the culture of the firm, not as a set of routines, but rather as a set of capabilities for receiving signals, interpreting and analysing them, and creatively working them out in the development of the firm.

NOTES

1. See, for example, Copeland, Koller and Murrin (1995).
2. Rappaport (1986) introduces more drastic simplifications: a constant unit operative margin (the ratio between the operating income and the sales), a constant rate of sales growth, etc.
3. Many authors underline the opportunity, from a practical point of view, to express cash flow on the basis of the most relevant economic variables used in the operating management of

the firm. See, for example, Grant (1998); Copeland, Koller and Murrin (1995); Rappaport (1986).

4. D'Aveni (1994) introduces the term *hyper competition* to indicate the new competition as the result of the dynamic strategic manoeuvres made by global rivals and innovators.

5. In an interview released by Bill Gates (CEO of Microsoft) in 1992, he commented: 'This is a hyper-competitive market. In this field dimensions are not always an advantage. On the contrary, ability and intelligence are. Success does not depend on company dimensions, rather on the determination used to pursue the subsequent competitive advantage' (*Business Week* 1992).

2. Main determinants of operating cash flows

INTRODUCTION AND OBJECTIVES

Operating earnings and cash flows principally depend on the structural characteristics of the firm and on its competitive positioning in relation to the competitive forces dominating the industry. From the positioning with respect to the competitive forces an advantage may result for the firm and therefore short-term positive earnings and cash flows.

In particular, the competitive advantage may take the form of a cost or a differentiation advantage, and it is the result of the specific firm structure and the competitive strategy adopted by the firm with respect to the rivals.

However the existing structure and positioning will not ensure positive earnings and cash flows in the long run, because of environmental changes and the dynamics of competitive forces. It will be necessary to plan structural transformation of the firm, to create new competitive advantages.

FIRM STRUCTURE AND OPERATING EARNINGS

First of all, the operating earnings (*EBITDA*) and cash flows depend on the characteristics of the firm's structure, that is the durable components and the features (activities) characterizing the firm's configuration and behaviour.[1] In particular, the characteristics of the existing structure of the firm, together with the conditions of factors and product markets, determine the revenues and the costs of the company (Dringoli 2000 and 2006).

More precisely, the production costs are affected by the technical coefficients of machines and plant, which cannot be significantly modified until a renewal/change of the technical structure is made.

Revenues are also affected by the qualitative features of the product and by the marketing structure of the firm. Given the sale price of the product $P(t)$ and the sale quantities $Q_V(t)$, total revenues $RT(t)$ in the period t (for example the year) are:

$$RT(t) = Q_v(t)\, P(t) \tag{2.1}$$

with t the basic time interval of reference (year).

In turn, the current operating costs (CT) are given by the sum of the costs of raw materials (CM), direct labour (CL), energy (CE), selling (CV) and administrative costs (CA), etc.:

$$CT(t) = CM(t) + CL(t) + CE(t) + CV(t) + CA(t) \qquad (2.2)$$

with:

$$CM(t) = Q_P(t)\, K_M\, P_M(t) \qquad (2.3)$$

$$CL(t) = Q_P(t)\, K_L\, P_L(t) \qquad (2.4)$$

$$CE(t) = Q_P(t)\, K_E\, P_E(t) \qquad (2.5)$$

where: $Q_P(t)$ is the quantity produced in period t; K_M, K_L, K_E are the technical coefficients of raw material, direct labour and energy, that is the quantities of different factors required to produce a unit of product.

The *EBITDA* results from the difference between the revenues and the operating costs previously mentioned:

$$EBITDA(t) = RT(t) - CT(t) \qquad (2.6)$$

Assuming the quantities sold Q_V are equal to the produced quantities $Q_P(t)$, in the period t, that is: [2]

$$Q_V(t) = Q_P(t) = Q(t) \qquad (2.7)$$

through the appropriate substitutions, we obtain:

$$EBITDA(t) = Q(t)P(t) - CM(t) - CL(t) - CE(t) - CV(t) - CA(t) \qquad (2.8)$$

And so:

$$EBITDA(t) = Q(t)\, P(t)\, [1 - K_M P_M/P(t) - K_L P_L/P(t) - K_E P_E/P(t) - C_V/P(t)$$

$$- C_A/P(t)\,] \qquad (2.9)$$

$$EBITDA(t) = Q(t)\, (P - C) \qquad (2.10)$$

with C_V, C_A the unit cost of selling and administration and $C = K_M P_M + K_L P_L (t) + K_E P_E$ the current operating unit cost.

These relationships highlight the influence of the existing structure of the firm on economic flows. It is clear that the lower the coefficients of raw materials (K_M), energy (K_E), and production workers (K_L), the higher the *EBITDA* will be.[3] This is also influenced by the terms of trade of the firm, that is the ratio of sale price (P) to price of factors $(P_M, P_L, P_E,$ etc.). Finally, the lower the sales and administration expenses are, the higher the *EBITDA* will be.

Therefore, given the firm's system, as its structural parameters $(K_M, K_E, K_L,$ etc.) stay constant in the short term, *EBITDA* depends on the relationships between cost and sale prices, and on the real production and sales volume, in relation to the sales and production capacity.

INDUSTRY STRUCTURE, COMPETITIVE POSITIONING AND OPERATING CASH FLOWS

The operating earnings depend on the existing competitive forces, in addition to the firm structure.

In particular, the sale price (P), the prices of raw materials and services (P_M), and the quantities of product sold (Q) are specifically affected by the conditions characterizing the product demand and competition among rivals.[4] These variables are furthermore influenced by the other actors in the competitive scenario, including potential entrants, manufacturers of substitute products, suppliers and buyers of the firm (Figure 2.1).[5]

The positioning of the firm in relation to the five competitive forces mentioned above triggers the intensity of the existing competitive pressure, and therefore the levels of sale prices, cost of factors and operating margin.

The Industry Competitors

The structure of the industry (number of competitors and concentration rate) deeply affects the level of sale prices and therefore the profits of the firm.

On this subject, remember that the *continuum* of competitive situations can be divided into four wide categories: perfect competition, imperfect or monopolistic competition, oligopoly and monopoly. To each of these, a different intensity of price competition is related. Table 2.1 shows that each category of competitive state is related to a range of the industry concentration index (HH Index).[6]

Obviously, these frameworks provide only some schemes of reference, which are not to be generalized.

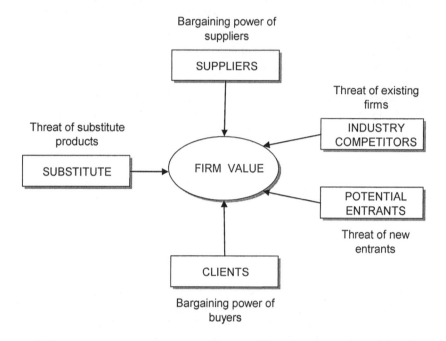

Figure 2.1   The five competitive forces threatening firm value

For example, sometimes there are cases of high competition also in the presence of only two competitors; or cases of low competition in markets characterized by multiple firms with differentiated products.

However, in general, rivalry among competitors increases and price levels shrink when:

- the number of competitors increases and they become more similar in terms of size and capability;
- the product demand increases slowly or stagnates;
- the industry conditions (for example the unemployed capacity) spur competitors to decrease prices or to use other competitive weapons in order to increase sale volumes;
- the switching from one brand to another is easy and not expensive.

Table 2.1   The effect of four categories of market structure on price competition

Type of competition	HH Index	Intensity of price competition
Perfect competition	Usually lower than 0.2	Fierce
Monopolistic competition	Usually lower than 0.2	May be fierce or weak depending on product differentiation
Oligopoly	From 0.2 to 0.6	May be fierce or weak depending on rivalry among different firms
Monopoly	From 0.6 and higher	Generally weak, unless there is the threat of new entrants

Source: adapted from Besanko, Dranove and Shanley (1996).

The Threat of New Entrants

The economic theory has highlighted the effects of new entrants, in addition to incumbents, on the level of prices and profits in oligopolistic markets. According to various authors, among them Bain (1956), Modigliani (1958) and Sylos Labini (1964), it would be the threat of potential entrants that would affect the conduct of oligopolistic firms in their price policies, rather than the action exerted by incumbents.

In other words, the oligopolistic firms would prefer to maintain lower prices and a wider product supply, in order to discourage the entry of new competitors. On the contrary, a policy of high prices would produce high profits in the short run, but it would favour the entry of new firms, attracted by the high profitability of the industry. In turn, the entry of new firms, by adding production capacity, would trigger a price reduction and therefore decrease the profits of all firms over a long period. So, the threat of new entrants represents an indirect competitive force that compels incumbents to decrease sale prices.

The effectiveness of such a force may be reduced by entry barriers to the sector, that is structural entry obstacles, established by the specific conditions of the industry.

It is common knowledge that entry barriers are mainly represented by:

- scale economies;
- product differentiation;
- cost advantages independent of scale.

Scale economies are entry barriers because they compel the new competitor to enter the business with a high minimum level of production scale, and therefore with a significant offering capacity, such as to determine a considerable post-entry price decrease (demand given). Post-entry price conditions can therefore diverge significantly from pre-entries and cause the annulment of extra profits favouring the entrance. So, scale economies tend to discourage the potential rival, creating a condition favourable to the incumbent (Besanko, Dranove and Shanley 1996). It has been demonstrated that the higher the ratio of the minimal efficient production scale to the total demand and the price elasticity of the demand, the higher the *limit price* and the profits of incumbents can be (Modigliani 1958; Sylos Labini 1964).

Product differentiation is an entry barrier because it is not sufficient for the entrant to build the production capacity and offer the product. It is necessary to significantly differentiate the product, in order to move already consolidated preferences. However, product differentiation is not easy: it requires investments, sometimes extremely high ones, the results of which are very uncertain by nature. On this point, think about the difficulties in entering the chocolate industry and competing against brands such as Ferrero, Mars, Lindt and others.

Cost advantages not depending on scale. Incumbents have advantages independently of their size. These are related to different factors, among which are control on scarce resources in the procurement (natural resources, raw materials) or sales markets (long-term or exclusive relationships with suppliers or customers), availability of patents or owned technologies, non-replicable production and distribution locations, experience and availability of a qualified labour force, any other market imperfection, or the amount and the cost of capital of new entrants compared to firms already operating in the industry.

The real extent of entry barriers determines the threat of new entrants and the sustainability of existing price levels and consequently of earnings.

Furthermore, among direct entry barriers, we have to consider the dissuasive power of the possible reaction to the potential entrance on the part of incumbent firms. This will depend on the amount of financial resources available and the capability of raising retaliations with relevant effects in the markets of possible competitors.

Summarizing, all these factors might represent a decisive obstacle to entering the industry. This will reinforce the monopoly power of incumbents and will favour higher prices.

Potential entrants may be:

- firms external to the product/market easily able to overcome the entry barriers;
- firms obtaining relevant synergies;
- clients and suppliers which would benefit from a vertical (upstream or downstream) integration of their activities.

The Threat of Substitute Products

Manufacturers of substitute products may represent a further important competitive force, capable of affecting the prices and profits of oligopolistic firms. Beyond certain price levels, in fact, the demand will move towards substitute products, causing a reduction of the firm's profit in the medium term. So, the existence of substitute products increases the price elasticity of the demand, since clients may move their demand towards substitute products each time the product price exceeds what they are likely to pay.

Obviously, if substitute products are not perfect, thanks to the product differentiation, the firm will have greater running control in prices and will be able to stably maintain higher profits. For example, the sugar industry competes against producers of artificial sweeteners; producers of glass bottles compete against manufacturers of plastic, paper, cardboard, and aluminium containers; producers of artificial fibres for the textile industry compete against producers of natural fibres, and so on.

The Bargaining Power of Suppliers

Suppliers may be considered a competitive force, since their bargaining power may increase the costs of raw materials, components and services, and reduce the margins and earnings of the buyer firm. In other words, suppliers, using their dealing power, may require changes of some elements of the supply relationship that are favourable to them: price increase, standardization of provided products, reduction of product variables, lengthening of delivery time, increase of minimum lot of order, reduction of assistance or design support, etc.[7]

Conditions favouring the increase of bargaining power of suppliers and of price-costs of factors are (Hax and Majluf 1984; Grant 1998):

- supply markets with few firms and which are more concentrated than industries of buyer firms;
- limited availability of substitute products to those of suppliers;
- small dimension of buyer firms compared with that of suppliers;
- significant contribution of supplier products to the quality of products of the buyer firm or to the efficiency of the production process;
- high differentiation of supplier products and/or high re-conversion costs;
- capability of suppliers to integrate downstream.

The Bargaining Power of Clients

Clients may be an important competitive force, since through their bargaining power they are able to compel the firm to make lower prices, in this way gaining a part of the value created by it. Very often, small and medium-sized manufacturers operating with a large client suffer the bargaining power of the client and accept lower prices.

In general, conditions increasing the bargaining power of clients are the following (Grant 1998):

- the purchasing market is concentrated;
- substitute products are available;
- re-conversion costs are low;
- products are not significant for the quality of the client's product;
- clients can integrate upstream;
- the threat of downstream integration is weak.

The industry structure in its broader form (Porter 1980), and therefore the intensity of competitive forces, significantly affects the level of sale prices, costs of factors and consequently also the operating earnings of the firm. The most relevant variables are:

- the number of competitors, their production capacities and the concentration rate of supply;
- the number of buyers, their purchase capacity and the concentration of demand;
- the degree of differentiation of products;
- the entry barriers, that is the relevant obstacles to entering the business, and the exit barriers;
- the number of substitute products;
- the relationship between the aggregate demand for the product and the whole production capacity;

- the growth rate of aggregate demand.

The relationship between the aggregate demand and the production capacity in the sector is of particular importance.

Unused production capacity is one of the critical factors forcing existing firms to compete on product prices. In particular, the higher the amount of fixed costs, compared with variable costs, the higher the propensity of firms to compete on prices. An aggressive strategy of price reduction for increasing sales volumes, and therefore reducing the excess capacity, can cause significant reductions of margins and operating earnings. Excess capacity can be the result of a decreasing rate of market growth and an excess of investments on the part of the firms.

The duration of the negative effects arising from an excess production capacity principally depends on exit barriers, that is the possibility of firms to exit the business and mobilize their resources to different businesses. When costs or barriers to the mobility of resources are high, it gets hard to exit the sector. So, the condition of having excess capacity, with its negative effects on prices and incomes, may last for a long time.

On the contrary, when the aggregate demand exceeds the production capacity of the industry, prices and incomes will be higher, as the result of weaker competition.

A further relevant characteristic of the industry structure, influencing prices and firm earnings, is the ratio between the aggregate demand and the minimal efficient scale of production. This influences the number of competitors able to conveniently operate in the market and significantly affects the conditions to entry in the industry, as highlighted by Modigliani (1958) and Sylos Labini (1964).[8]

Finally, the firm's performance is deeply affected by the growth rate of the aggregate demand of products and services. Businesses characterized by a low growth rate usually show a greater rivalry among competitors and lower profitability in the long run.

On the other hand, opposite considerations count in sectors characterized by high growth rates (Thompson and Strickland 1998).

Summarizing, firm's earnings and cash flows are affected by the industry structure. The competitive pressure acting on the firm depends on its positioning in relation to the five competitive forces examined above. In particular, the positioning in relation to clients, incumbents, new entrants and substitute products affects the price level and sales volumes obtained by the firm; while the positioning with respect to suppliers affects the variable unit costs and therefore the operative fixed costs. When the competitive positioning in relation to the five competitive forces is weak, the firm will obtain low margins and low income flows.

Conversely, when the firm is adequately positioned with respect to the competitive forces, for example when clients and suppliers show a weak bargaining power, there are no good substitutes for the product, there are high entry barriers to the industry, and rivalry among existing firms is moderate, the firm will achieve high margins and high earnings.

To compete successfully, the entrepreneur will have to configure the structure of the firm so as to emphasize the differential elements compared with competitors, achieving a strong and certain competitive advantage.

BUILDING THE FIRM STRUCTURE AND THE COMPETITIVE POSITIONING TO CREATE VALUE

Existing competitors play a major role among forces affecting the performance of the firm. Therefore it is particularly relevant for the firm to create an adequate positioning in relation to existing rivals, in order to gain a competitive advantage. On this subject, the competitive advantage may be of three different forms: cost advantage, differentiation advantage or cost–differentiation advantage.

The cost advantage arises when the firm succeeds in organizing more efficiently the activities for manufacturing and selling the product, so that the product costs less, even if it is basically equal to competitors' products.

The differentiation advantage depends on the greater benefits provided by the product, compared with those offered by competitors. This may derive from the greater ability to satisfy customer needs, through more appreciated attributes. In this case, a significant premium price emerges or a larger sales volume, at equal prices (Porter 1980 and 1985; Grant 1998).[9]

The cost–differentiation advantage arises when a firm is capable of gaining competitive advantage by offering two types of value to customers, some differentiated features (but fewer than those provided by the product-differentiated firm) and at a relatively low cost, but not as low as the products of the low-cost leader (Hitt, Ireland and Hoskisson 1997; Dess et al. 1995).

The cost advantage may result from different factors: input costs, operating efficiency, scale economies, employment capabilities and competencies, outsourcing of some production activities, etc. For example, it is known that companies such as Nike and Reebok created competitive advantages with respect to their rivals, through the decentralization of manufacturing to firms operating in Thailand, China and the Philippines, and the focusing of internal activities on R&D, design, distribution, etc.

The differentiation advantage may derive from different factors: the innovation of products or services, distribution and logistic activities and brand policies, so as to qualify the supply of the firm in comparison with that of competitors. The differentiation advantage allows value leveraging to be created on the product, in terms of quality or image, so that customers are willing to pay a premium price or to buy higher quantities.

The cost advantage enables the firm to create value by selling at lower prices a product which is more or less equal to those of competitors, thereby obtaining higher sale volumes.

The cost–differentiation advantage derives both from product differentiation and cost leadership; product differentiation leads to premium prices at the same time that cost leadership implies lower costs.

For creating value, the structure of the firm must be configured so as to offer real advantages, in terms of costs or differentiation or a combination of them, in comparison with competitors. In the first case, the firm will succeed in establishing lower prices and will create value through higher volumes of production and sales. In the second case, leveraging on product differentiation, the firm will be able to establish a higher price for the product, with higher unit margins. In the third case the firm will benefit from combined forms of premium price and low cost and higher volumes.

In short, firms creating value through low costs are 'structurally' different from firms basing their competitiveness on product differentiation or on a combined form of low cost and differentiation. The diversity concerns, in particular, the production and marketing structure and the positioning in the market.

The performance achieved by the firm, in terms of operating earnings and cash flow, demonstrates the effectiveness of the existing competitive positioning and the validity of the firm's structure, in relation to the environmental conditions.

ENVIRONMENTAL CHANGES, PROGRESSIVE EROSION OF COMPETITIVE ADVANTAGE AND OPERATING CASH FLOWS

The existing firm structure and the competitive positioning cannot ensure positive earnings and cash flows in the long run, because of environmental changes.

Changes may concern products and processes, industry concentration rate, threat of substitute products, level of entry barriers, scale economies, growth of aggregate demand, etc. These changes are the result both of factors outside the industry and of evolution forces acting inside it.

Therefore, the competitive advantage of the firm over competitors is *temporary* (D'Aveni 1994). Differential benefits provided to consumers tend to decrease, due to the introduction of new product types and models on the part of rivals, represented by more dynamic and newer firms.[10] The advantages in terms of costs tend also to shrink or to turn into cost disadvantages, as long as competitors continue to introduce new plant and machinery incorporating technical progress acquired during that time.

The car, pharmaceutical, electronics and microprocessor industries offer extensive evidence of firms having suffered the strong erosion of competitive advantages by continuous innovations of products and processes. On this topic see the section Strategy Focus at the end of this chapter.

CREATING NEW COMPETITIVE ADVANTAGES AND INCREASING CASH FLOWS THROUGH INNOVATION

It will be necessary to plan structural transformations of the firm, innovating processes and products, so as to successfully cope with the evolution of the environment and the new competitive forces, thereby creating new sources of competitive advantage. In particular, the structural change will have to be compliant with the environment changes, so that sufficient earnings and cash flows can be gained, in relation to the invested capital.

In general, the prevailing dynamics of the industry spur the firm to pursue a certain strategy for recovering the competitive advantage. For example, in the cement industry, product standardization prevents the industry from implementing differentiation and product innovation strategies. In this industry the competitive strategy is mandatory: it consists of productivity increases not lower than the industry average. This will be possible by means of technical progress and scale economies in production. We come up with similar situations in the paper, steel, glass, and other commodities industries.

On the other hand, in high technology industries, the fundamental trend is represented by technical progress incorporated in new products, the performances of which are superior to the previous ones. Also in this case, the competitive strategy is mandatory: it consists of production innovations, to be achieved quickly and systematically. Consider what has been happening in the microprocessor, software, new materials and pharmaceutical industries.

In other industries, both productivity increases and changes in the tastes and needs of consumers are important. Think about the car and appliance industries, where no radical product innovations have been introduced, but where there has been a continuum of incremental innovations either in products or in production processes. In these sectors, the strategy to create value is hybrid: achieving both the renewal of product types and models and productivity improvement at least equal to the average of the industry.

In general, the choice of the strategy is determined by the changing forces prevailing in the industry where the firm operates. However, it is necessary to evaluate, case by case, if there are the conditions for a strategy of structural development that really can increase the value of the firm.

STRATEGY FOCUS: TEMPORALITY OF COMPETITIVE ADVANTAGE IN HIGHLY COMPETITIVE INDUSTRIES

In highly competitive industries attempting to sustain an old advantage can be of negative value. Attempting to sustain an old advantage can eat up resources that should be used to generate the next move, thereby inviting attack from savvy competitors. In highly competitive industries the better defence is often a strong offence, by innovation.

The Case of Digital Equipment

Despite the fact that it happened many years ago, the case of Digital Equipment Corporation (DEC) is still emblematic. DEC tried to sustain its advantage in minicomputers. It had posted a 31% average growth rate from 1977 to 1982 by focusing on minicomputers. But the company clung so tenaciously to its advantage in minicomputers that it failed to develop a strong position in the emerging markets for microcomputers and personal computers. As CEO K. Olsen commented in a 1984 *Business Week* article, 'We had six PCs in the house that we could have launched in the late 70s. But we were selling so many VAX minicomputers, it would have been immoral to chase a new market'.

By 1992, *Business Week* notes, DEC had 'ousted' Olsen and taken $3.1 billion in charges over two years, cut 18,000 staff and closed 165 facilities. Its pursuit of a sustainable advantage may have left it without the series of temporary advantages it needed to thrive in a hypercompetitive market, where competitors just destroyed Digital's advantage by outmanoeuvring it.[11]

The Case of Xerox

In the 1970s, Xerox achieved a net advantage in relation to its rivals, thanks to the development of a new technological platform (xerographyelectrograph) for copying machines. The new model was introduced in 1964, using a different technology that was easier to use, compared with the existing machines. Consequently, the sales of the firm increased rapidly as did the profits with them. In 1965, sales were ten times higher than first year sales; in 1969, profits increased 600%, from 23 million dollars in 1964 to 161 million. Furthermore, the new platform let Xerox enter new promising businesses such as PCs and office automation.

At the end of the 1970s, the competitive advantage of Xerox did not exist any more. It had been eroded by the entry of new Japanese firms, favoured by the expiration of the greater part of patents and by the introduction of new models and technologies on the part of competitors, with a 25% price reduction compared with Xerox products. From 94% in 1970, the Xerox market share shrank to 41% in the 1980s. All this despite the strength of the brand and of the commercial organization.

In the 1990s, competition in the copying machines market became fiercer and fiercer with further decreases in Xerox market shares, reaching 26%, and the consequent crisis of the company. The firm which had built an extremely strong competitive position through technological innovation did not succeed in sustaining it, or to keep on benefiting from its competitive advantage.

As long as the market moved towards digital copying machines and network solutions, the firm found itself faced with competitors ready to exploit the technological opportunities, such as Canon and HP (Wonglimpiyarat 2004).

The Case of Caterpillar

In 1981 Caterpillar controlled more than 50% of the world market for earth moving equipment. It was the world's largest manufacturer of these products, with sales close to 9 billion dollars. In that period Komatsu was the dominant company in Japan, but it held only 16% of the world market. By 1984 Komatsu's share of the world market had grown to 25% and Caterpillar's had dropped to 43%. This was the result of aggressive competition constantly directed at disrupting Caterpillar's competitive advantage, based on full line quality products, strong service and support, high global volume and low cost (economies of scale).

The success of Komatsu's action was founded on an aggressive strategy of innovations: the development of new technology made it possible to drive down the costs of the existing products and the ability to roll out a series of new products made possible to chip away the Caterpillar's market and to outpace it in the new markets (D'Aveni 1994).

The Case of IBM

During the 1980s in the PC industry, IBM had developed a strong competitive advantage with entry barriers and power over buyers and suppliers that extended for years. But during the 1990s the life cycles of products were reduced by new competitors and maintaining a sustainable advantage became increasingly difficult. Advantages in cost and quality were progressively eroded by the actions of new firms. Even seemingly unbeatable advantages such as brand, technology, geographic or market entry barriers and deep pockets were proving to be no match for the new aggressive and innovative competitors.

Since 2001 IBM has been losing money in its personal computing division. To rebuild its competitive advantage IBM had moved all manufacturing of the desktop PCs to SanminaSCI, a global supplier providing contract manufacturing services to a number of brand-name firms. The laptops were assembled in Mexico, Scotland and China. But none of these moves had been enough to make PCs a profitable business. On 7 December 2004 IBM announced the sale of its personal computer division to Lenovo, a Chinese computer manufacturer. The sale is the symbol of the end of an era for an American company that had pioneered personal computing. The revolutionary innovation that IBM introduced into American life 23 years earlier with its Personal Computer had finally reached commodity status. Personal computers can now be made all over the world and the margins have become vanishingly thin. In any personal computer much of the value of the product comes not from the brand name but rather from components purchased from no-name suppliers.

In this changed environment, an information technology company has two radical options for rebuilding a competitive advantage and creating value: invest heavily in R&D and be a high-value innovation provider for enterprises, or differentiate by leveraging vast economies of scale, high volumes and low price. IBM chose the first route; it decided to withdraw from making a commodity and refocus on the more profitable business of services and high-end hardware: software for systems solutions, servers and specialized components (Berger 2005). On the other hand, other IT companies are expanding their commodity business.

The Case of Borders

In March 2008 Borders, the second bookstore chain in the USA, announced the suspension of the dividend and gave JP Morgan and Merrill Lynch the task to explore strategic alternatives: selling the entire group or some activities. This decision was the consequence of a continuously declining market share eroded by new competitors such as Wal-Mart and on-line distributors.

The innovations in distribution by these new competitors have rapidly disrupted the competitive advantage of Borders, based on market and geographic entry barriers, brand image and a large established selling network. In 2007, after two years of losses, the company recorded a 66% fall in share price, a liquidity shortage and a strong increasing debt, even threatening its survival (*Il Sole–24Ore*, 21 March 2008).

NOTES

1. We consider the firm as a complex system of interrelated activities performed to reach a purpose. The mix and the configuration of these activities *cannot be modified continuously*; they are irreversible in the short term, for economic reasons (Dringoli 1995, 2000). The concept of *structure* is largely used in management literature. On this topic, see: Chandler (1969), Ceccanti (1996) and Mintzberg (1983, 1990). This author points out: 'Structure may be malleable, but it cannot be altered at will just because a leader has conceived a new strategy. Many organizations have come to grief over just such a belief' (1990, p. 183). Without using the term structure, Ghemawat (1991) underlines the tendency of organizations to persist over time with their respective strategies (commitment) and specifies four processes causing the strategic persistence: lock in, lock out, lags and inertia. In short, this author points out that a firm persists in its initial strategy because it remains locked into its durable and specific factors, the delay in adapting them to the desired levels and the inertia of organizations. The concept of firm structure is implicit in his concept of commitment: his sticky factors are those we name structural components of a firm, that is durable, specialized, non-transferable factors. Thus, affirming that commitment is the only general explanation for sustained differences in the performance of organizations, means reckoning that the different performances between firms are caused by different structures.
2. This hypothesis means product stocks remain unchanged in the period T.
3. These production coefficients are the reciprocals of productivity indexes. The higher the latter, the lower the coefficients and the consumption of production factors are. The *labour productivity index*, for example, is given by: $1/K_L$; the higher this index is, the lower the labour coefficient K_L.
4. On the relations between the performance of the firm and the industry structure, see: Rumelt (1986); Scherer and Ross (1990); Besanko, Dranove and Shanley (1996).
5. On this topic see: Porter (1980); Hitt, Ireland and Hoskisson (1997).
6. This is referred to as the Herfindahl-Hirshman index; it equals the sum of the squared market shares of all firms in the market. For its mathematical structure the HH index represents a more informative measure than the N-firm concentration ratio.
7. This vision of the firm–supplier relationship as a competitive relationship, highlighted also by Porter (1980), cannot be generalized. In the last few years the view of suppliers as partners has been consolidated. The importance of collaborative relationships, based on mutual benefits among actors forming the industry value chain or the value constellation, is a relevant phenomenon in many sectors, where stable and continuing relationships between suppliers and clients become extremely important for obtaining the market leadership.

8. As known, we talk about natural monopoly when the market demand is insufficient for more than one firm operating on an efficient minimal scale. On this topic, see Besanko, Dranove and Shanley (1996).
9. Porter considers cost leadership and differentiation strategies mutually excludible: 'firms trying to pursue both, risk ending up "stuck in the middle". For these firms the almost certain result is low profitability. Either they lose clients which ensure high volumes, or they assist in the volatilization of the greatest part of profits in the attempt to compete with firms with lower costs. At the same time, they will lose also those clients that ensure higher margins − the cream of the market − leaving them to firms that have focused on higher margin segments or that have succeeded in a substantial differentiation. The firm that stops in the middle of the ford has probably a less defined business culture, and operates in a conflicting organizational and motivational structure' (Porter 1980, p. 42).
10. On the continuous erosion of competitive advantage, see also Mueller (1986); Day (1999); Day and Reibstein (1997).
11. On this subject see D'Aveni (1994, p. 9).

3. Fundamental environment trends and innovation strategies

INTRODUCTION AND OBJECTIVES

The competitive advantage achieved by a firm and its consequent positive earning flows are temporary, since the evolution of the environment makes the existing firm's structure 'old' in terms of processes and products, as time passes by, in comparison with those of more advanced competitors.

Also the entry barriers to an industry represent increasingly weak obstacles and often break down suddenly under the impact of rapid changes in the technologies of the information era, enabling the advancement of more innovative firms.

To rebuild the competitive advantage and to continue creating value, it is necessary to modify the existing structure of the firm, according to development strategies in compliance with the evolutionary trends of the environment.

In this chapter we propose three development models for increasing the value of the firm, with reference to prevailing trends in highly competitive industries.

THE FUNDAMENTAL CHANGING FORCES OF COMPETITIVE CONDITIONS

Understanding which factors are the main changing forces in the industry is of fundamental importance for defining the strategy to create value.[1] This not only permits identifying the changes of firm structure needed to meet the new competitive conditions of the industry, but also achieving them on time, so as to rebuild the competitive advantage and increase the value of the firm.

Indeed, a development strategy should be a succession of structural changes to be accomplished in the long run, in order to continue creating value.

In our opinion, the main forces that modify the conditions of competition in the most important industries are the following:

- technical progress related to machinery and plant and changes in the minimal efficient production scale (scale economies);
- technical progress and product innovation;
- changes in customer tastes, behaviour and lifestyle.

Technical Progress Embodied in New Machines and Plant

Innovation in production processes is a fundamental changing factor of competitive conditions of an industry. This may cause significant increases in labour productivity, with relevant effects on costs and therefore on product prices, favouring the most innovative firm and triggering the conditions to remove inefficient firms from the industry. The consequence is greater industry concentration and the evolution of the market towards oligopolistic forms. Process innovations may produce increases or decreases in scale economies and influence the vertical integration degree.

Innovation which produces significant scale economies will favour the growth of firms and the concentration of industry. It will push ahead strategies based on cost reduction and, in the meantime, it will reinforce the entry barriers to the industry. The opposite happens if innovation reduces the efficient scale of production. Finally, innovation or/and increasing production scale may favour the internationalization and the globalization of the industry.

Technical Progress and Product Innovation

Product innovation is the most important source of change in industries. It increases the differentiation of products and reduces the competition, increasing the competitive advantage of innovating firms. When product innovation is able to be protected from imitations, it creates durable competitive advantages, also limiting the competitiveness of new entrants.

Changes in Consumer Tastes, Behaviour and Lifestyle

In some industries demand is influenced by lifestyle, tastes, culture and the social conditions of buyers. Think about the effects of increasing leisure time, mobility, attention to health and the new role of women within society, etc.

Changes in tastes and consumers' behaviour are a powerful factor of competition in an industry. They may be an advantage to the most dynamic firm, capable of foreseeing and rapidly adapting its structure, through product differentiation policies and renewal of product types and models.

Alternatively, they can cause the decline of more conservative firms, incapable of quickly changing the products they offer.

There are also non-economic forces which may exert a significant influence on the results of a firm. Among them, consider the government policies directed at controlling the entry of new competitors, through authorization procedures of licensing, and norms for controlling prices. The first may limit the entry of new firms and give protection to the existing firms. The latter may offer a protective umbrella to less efficient firms, limiting competition or creating conditions unfavourable to firms already operating in the business, so as to facilitate their exit.

We will focus on the economic forces capable of modifying the existing competitive system and compelling the firm to adopt more challenging and risky strategies for changing its structure.

INDUSTRY MODELS AND INNOVATION STRATEGIES FOR CREATING VALUE

The environment and in particular the industry in which the firm operates are subject to long-term changes, offering relevant opportunities for firms which are attentive and ready to modify their existing structure.

However, these changes may also cancel the achieved competitive advantage and even cause irreversible crises for those firms not implementing adequate structural developments. For example, in industries characterized by a continuous flow of product innovations, the firm which maintains its products unchanged will in time suffer a progressive erosion of sales and a progressive reduction in earnings, with the consequent destruction of value.[2]

When environmental changes are systematic and non-reversible, policies directed at defending and maintaining the achieved competitive advantage will only offer a temporary and partial solution to the problem. The firm will have to change its structure, in order to obtain higher levels of productivity and to offer new products for recovering the competitive advantage eroded by the aggressive action of rivals. To this purpose, it will be necessary to implement investments in new 'equipment', characterized by higher productivity and/or greater production capacity and investments in new products, capable of recovering the market position.

Identifying the dominating trends of the industry is, therefore, of major importance to correctly defining the strategy of structural development suitable for creating value.

In general, industries are influenced by various changing forces, but only some of them are capable of significantly modifying the conditions of competition. Therefore, the leading firm will have to base its development strategy on the major environment trends, in order to create value.

To examine these subjects carefully and concentrate our analysis on the most relevant topics, we have identified three models of industries (Table 3.1).[3]

Table 3.1   Models of industries and innovation strategies

Types of industry	Driving forces	Innovation strategies
Industries with basically homogeneous products	Technical progress embodied in new production processes	*Dominant strategy*: Renewal of plant or endogenous innovation of production technologies *Objective*: Productivity increase
Industries with differentiated products and radical product innovations	Change in consumers' tastes and behaviour, technical progress	*Dominant strategy* : Innovation of product *Objective*: Recovery of market potential and creation of new markets
Industries with differentiated products	Technical progress embodied in new production processes and change of consumers' tastes and behaviour	*Dominant strategy*: Renewal of plant or endogenous innovation of production technologies and product innovation *Objective:* Productivity increase and recovery of market potential

Source: Dringoli (2007).

The first model is represented by industries characterized by substantially homogeneous products, where fundamental trends are represented by process innovations caused by the technical progress embodied in new plant and production processes (type A industries). These innovations induce increases in factor productivity and the consequent reductions in costs and prices. That shrinks the operating earnings of firms maintaining the old production structures (Figure 3.1).

Since technical progress, embodied in new capital equipment, undercuts operating costs with the new methods, firms must compete mainly on costs. The strategy to be adopted consists in increasing the productivity levels of factors (capital and labour), through investment in new plant. We refer, for example, to industries such as steel, paper, cement, oil refining, and other commodities.

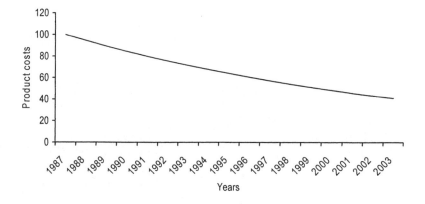

Note: Productivity increases in the steel industry and operating costs of equipment
         incorporating the best modern technologies (5.4% per year 1987–2003).

Source: Author's elaboration on US Department of Labor data (2006).

Figure 3.1   Fundamental trends in type A industries: process innovations
and decline of operating costs

The second model (type B industries) is represented by industries characterized by product innovations, where the main environmental trends are both the change in consumers' tastes and behaviour and the innovation of products.

In these industries the life of an existing product is quickly reduced and ended, because technical progress and the change in customers' demand shift preferences to new products, causing the fall of old product sales (Figure 3.2). The renewal of product types and models is the winning strategy.

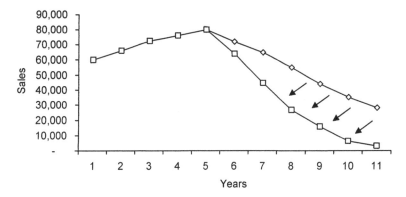

Figure 3.2   Fundamental trends in type B industries: product innovations and reduction of product life cycle

Product innovation can be radical in industries characterized by rapid technical progress and a big advancement of scientific knowledge. We mainly refer to the so-called 'science-based' industries, such as the pharmaceutical, information technology and biotech industries. In these industries, the strategy for creating value by product innovation also requires planning high investment in R&D activities.

The third model (type C industries) is represented by industries where both process and product innovation are important. They are characterized by significant increases in productivity and short-life products. In these industries, in order to create value, the firm has to carry out an integrated strategy, pursuing productivity improvement and production innovation together. We refer, for example, to industries such as the automobile, appliances and consumer electronics industries, etc.

We want to point out that the innovation strategy presents distinctive features, with regard to changes in existing firm structure. In some cases, these changes will involve only the production system, in other cases they will also involve the marketing and logistics system, or the whole firm system. However, it is important to highlight that the part of the firm system that we named firm's structure is irreversible in the short run (Ghemawat 1991; Dringoli 1995, 2007). First, this is because changes involve specific tangible and intangible durable factors which are difficult to negotiate, and which trigger the use of consistent financial resources that cannot be recovered in the short term. Second, the achievement of positive results requires stabilization of operating and marketing processes, in order to fully deploy the learning and diffusion processes. As long as cumulative production increases, numerous opportunities arise to reduce costs, making better use of raw materials and components. All this happens because the entire organization simply learns to do better. This phenomenon is represented by *learning curves* or experience effects, which highlight product costs decreasing at a constant rate each time the cumulative volume of production doubles.[4]

For all these reasons, after the change in the existing structure resulting from new equipment or new products, the firm is 'forced' to maintain processes and operating cycles, which are constant for a 'discrete period', continuing the strategic pattern, thereby enabling the full exploitation of the investments. Consequently, strategic changes must not be made continuously, but at 'discrete' intervals of time, according to a long-term vision of industry demand and supply, estimating costs and benefits of investments.

STRATEGY FOCUS: FUNDAMENTAL TRENDS OF THE ENVIRONMENT IN SOME RELEVANT INDUSTRIES

In our opinion the main forces that modify the conditions of competition in the most important industries are the following:

1. technical progress related to machinery and plant and changes in the minimal efficient production scale;
2. technical progress and product innovation;
3. changes in customer tastes, behaviour and lifestyle.

These forces progressively erode the competitive advantage of firms. The technical progress related to machinery and plant increases the productivity of production factor, primarily labour productivity, causing a reduction in the operating costs of innovative firms and the consequent decline in product prices. The technical progress related to products improves the performance and boosts sales of new products, reducing the sales and the operating earnings of firms still operating with old structures and products.

Understanding these evolutionary trends and the intensity of change is the base for designing the strategy and rebuilding a competitive advantage.

Technological Progress and Labour Productivity Increases

In Table 3.2 data are shown on labour productivity trends in some important industries. They clearly point out the temporality of the competitive advantage for a successful firm and the need of a process innovation strategy for increasing labour productivity and sustaining the firm's value.

This is true, in particular, for firms operating in some industries, characterized in these years by very high rates of increase in labour productivity, such as computers and semiconductors.

Table 3.2   Yearly growth rate of labour productivity (output per hour) in 1987–2004

Industry	Yearly growth rate 1987–2004 (%)
Oil products	3.2
Basic chemistry	2.7
Paper	3.4
Plastics	2.7
Resins, rubber, and artificial fibres	2.8
Steel factories and metal alloy products	5.4
Industrial machinery	3.0
Appliances	4.6
Medical systems	3.8
Motor vehicles	3.8
Components of motor vehicles	3.4
Computers and electronics	13.5
Computers and peripherals	24.1
Communication equipment	7.8
Audio and video equipment	8.4
Semiconductors and electronics	19.7
Electronic equipment	4.2

Source: US Department of Labor (2006); see also Russel, Takac and Usher (2004).

Technological Progress and the Shortening of the Product Life Cycle

In some industries product innovations are the fundamental force changing the competitive positioning of the firm and affecting the operating earnings and firm value. Among these industries are pharmaceuticals, cars, computers and electronics, appliances and many others.

Life cycles of products are continuously reduced by technical innovations and by the style and behaviour changes of customers; all these force firms to innovate and change their firm structures.

Product innovation is the main competitive weapon in the car industry. In Figure 3.3 we show the life cycles of some important models of cars from the Fiat Company.

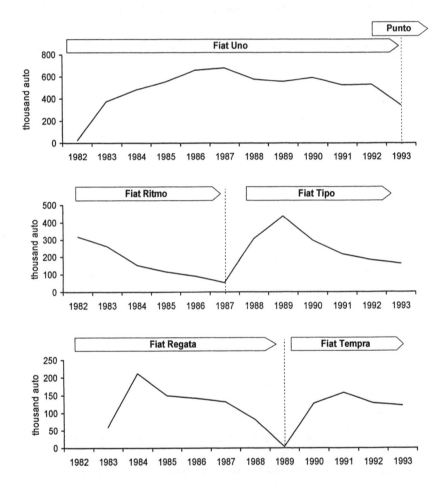

Source: Author's elaboration on data from ANFIA, Turin, 1994.

Figure 3.3   The life cycles of some car models (yearly production)

You can see the declining of product sales after a certain period of time, the length of which depends on the success of the model previously launched and the pressure from competitors, through the introduction of new products and models.

A clear vision of the fundamental environmental trends (for example the expected rate of increment of labour productivity or the duration of a product's life cycle in the industry) allows the management to define the direction of structural changes to carry out, the type of innovation to search for and the time to introduce it, for creating new value.

Technical progress and product innovation is the fundamental force changing the competitive edge also in the pharmaceutical industry.

Competition in the development of new pharmaceuticals is intense since all pharmaceutical companies are searching for effective and cost-efficient medicines. The sharply rising resource requirements to access the full range of new technologies, particularly following the decoding of the human genome, has been one reason for industry consolidation, as well as for the increase in collaboration between major pharmaceutical companies and specialized niche players at the forefront of their particular field.

It is known that product innovations in this industry are characterized by a long, expensive and risky process. With regard to the innovation process for obtaining a new drug, two macro phases can be identified: the drug discovery and the development of the new product. Drug discovery includes the basic research, screening activities and synthesis of the new chemical entity (NCE); the development is the activity for transformation of the NCE into a drug and it includes all pre-clinical and clinical activities to test its effectiveness.

In particular clinical trials are conducted to determine whether or not a new drug or treatment is both safe and effective in people. These research studies rely on patients who voluntarily participate and try a new drug or treatment. Some of these drugs have not yet been approved by international health authorities. Most clinical trials that involve the testing of a new drug follow a series of steps, called phases.

Usually the process for a new drug requires four clinical phases. In phase I, researchers test a new drug or treatment in a small group of people (20–80) for the first time to evaluate its safety, determine a safe dosage range and identify side effects. In phase II the study drug or treatment is given to a larger group of people (100–300) to see if it is effective and to further evaluate its safety.

In phase III, the study drug or treatment is given to large groups of people (1000–3000) to confirm its effectiveness, monitor side effects, compare it to commonly used treatments and collect information that will allow the drug or treatment to be used safely. In phase IV post-marketing studies delineate additional information including the drug's risks, benefits and optimal use.

The probability of technical success of a new pharmaceutical product is very low in comparison with the other sectors. In particular the risks of abandoning the product are very high in the initial phases of research; only a few compounds go on to the development phases. These are the more expensive phases which take longer.

According to recent studies the whole R&D process for a new chemical entity (NCE) lasts on average 14 years; instead the development cycle of new drugs, such as new compounds or dosages, is shorter. The required R&D investment is estimated at approximately $800–1000 million for an NCE and $150–200 million for a new compound or dosage (Barral 1997; Di Masi 1991).

NOTES

1. On this topic, see Hofer and Schendel (1978); Hamel and Prahalad (1994, pp. 72–77).
2. The role of innovation in a market economy has been highlighted by Schumpeter (1942) with the expression 'creative destruction'. According to Schumpeter, what really counts is not competition on price at a certain date, but rather competition spurred by new products, new technologies, and new organizational solutions.
3. The importance of understanding the evolution of industries has been emphasized by many authors. The traditional paradigm used in strategy studies is the industry life cycle; on this topic see Porter (1980) and Grant (1998). We also mention the new theories on the ecology of organizations, according to which the industry evolution is the result of a Darwinian selection process (Carroll and Hannan 2000). Among the most recent studies with an operative approach see McGahan (2004). This author emphasizes four different types of environment changes: radical, progressive, creative and intermediating.
4. On the learning curves see Boston Consulting Group (1972); Abernaty (1978); Hayes and Weelwright (1984); Mariotti and Migliarese (1984); Lieberman (1984); Ghemawat (1985); Ross (1986); Hill (1987).

4. Creating value through process innovation strategies

INTRODUCTION AND OBJECTIVES

In industries characterized by continuous technological innovations in productive processes, firms maintaining their structures unchanged suffer from a progressive deterioration of operating cash flows, up to the point of experiencing negative values. If a firm wants to remain in the market and receive an adequate return on its capital, it has to change its technical structure in order to increase the productivity of inputs, especially labour.

To identify the innovation strategy capable of creating value, it is necessary, first of all, to carefully estimate the environment dynamics. With this aim in mind, we will analyse the relationships between all relevant variables and propose a quantitative model for evaluating the strategy, under the hypotheses both of exogenous and endogenous technical progress.

The model defines the conditions under which a strategy of process innovation can create value, linking the decision concerning the new investment to the rate of productivity improvement, the rate of salary increase, the rate of plant efficiency reduction, the cost of capital and the capital intensity. The model also underlines the importance of industry structure on product prices and thus on strategy value.

TECHNICAL PROGRESS AND EROSION OF OPERATING CASH FLOWS

In this chapter we refer to industries where the main environment trends are indicated by the innovations in production processes, while products remain basically unchanged. This is what happens in some industries such as steel, paper, oil products, basic chemistry, artificial fibres, resins, plastics, industrial equipment, etc. In other different industries innovations in industrial processes go along with product innovation, such as in the video equipment industry, computers, electronics, computer accessories, semiconductors, appliances, and motor vehicles.

The effects of technological innovations on a firm's outcome are relevant; they mainly consist in reduction of labour per unit of product, that is in the increase of labour productivity, and in a reduction of energy, raw materials and services per unit of product.

In these industries, a firm renewing its plant operates with modern equipment, incorporating the technological progress achieved until that date, with a high hourly productivity.[1] But, as time passes by, this firm will sustain an increasing cost per product, due to the increasing expenses of maintenance and recovery of equipment and plant. Most of all, its production structure becomes more and more out-of-date, due to the flow of new techniques incorporated in more recent machinery.

While this firm will not be capable of substituting its equipment in the short term, by continuing to operate with this equipment it will not be capable of benefiting from the emerging technical progress, since this is incorporated into new machinery. Therefore, it will sustain an increasing unit cost per product, caused by the growth rate of salaries and the physical deterioration of plant, while other competing firms, operating with more modern equipment, will have lower operating costs by means of higher productivity.

Competition driven by cost reduction will determine a decrease in product prices and therefore a progressive erosion of the unit margin of the firm until it has negative earnings and cash flows.[2] Under these conditions, the firm has to define a strategy for renewing its production structure, in order to obtain higher productivity of factors and lower costs.

The importance of process innovation for the competitiveness of firms emerges with great evidence from the experience of many firms. The case of the Italian ceramic tiles industry (for floors and walls) is emblematic of this, where the continuous flow of process innovations (automatic presses, rapid cooking kilns and related upstream and downstream automatic equipment) determined significant increases in labour productivity and significant decreases in energy consumption (Bursi 1984; Russo 1996). This is illustrated in the Strategy Focus at the end of this Chapter.

Similar productivity dynamics were seen in industries such as those of colorant chemistry, paper, and steel.

EXOGENOUS TECHNICAL PROGRESS AND PROCESS INNOVATION STRATEGY THROUGH INVESTMENTS IN NEW PLANT AND EQUIPMENT

In industries characterized by a continuous flow of innovations in production processes, the firm renewing its production structure will be capable of producing with lower unit costs and higher margins and incomes.

But, as time passes by, other firms will renew their plant or will enter the market with more and more efficient plant, causing the progressive contraction of the net income flows of our firm.[3] In fact, at the beginning of its lifetime, each 'new plant' is modern and its production per hour of labour is higher than the average of similar units operating in the industry. But, during the rest of its lifetime the plant becomes more and more out-of-date, because of new technological solutions, incorporated into more recent equipment.

The firm endowed with the more recent plant will obtain a higher gross margin per product unit, but this margin will decrease, as long as new techniques and new plant are available. This will happen since, in competitive conditions, product prices will follow the reduction of costs made possible by the new production techniques.

The time will come when the existing production structure will not provide any more advantages and will be substituted. To be precise, the change in the technical structure cannot be put off until after the date the firm's cash flow moves from positive to negative. That is the time at which the decreasing product price will become lower than the unit operating cost.

It might be convenient to anticipate the change of the production structure only if the new configuration is capable of generating gross income flows, such as compensating for the losses from the anticipated cut of the previous investment (dropping or dismantling of the plant).

In general, existing plants have the possibility to survive *pro tempore* even if they are surpassed. The disadvantage of using higher quantities of factors than those required by the best standards is more than balanced by the fact that the cost of investment has already been sustained (sunk cost). In other words, if production with modern technologies gives a cost advantage, it is necessary to sustain an additional cost – the cost of the new plant – in order to obtain it.

So, even if the sector is characterized by a continuous flow of technique changes, each firm will change its structure after a 'discrete' interval of time, due to the existing investments and their irreversibility in the short run.

A MODEL FOR ESTIMATING THE VALUE OF PROCESS INNOVATION STRATEGIES

To evaluate a strategy of process innovation and identify the key variables, we will consider technical progress exogenous to the firm and technical progress embodied in new capital equipment.

Technical progress exogenous to the firm means the technological innovations to be realized by external firms specialized in the production of 'machines'. This hypothesis will be removed later, when considering technical progress endogenous to the firm, that is technical progress that is realized by the same firm that uses it, producing innovation through research and development activities.

Regarding the second hypothesis (technical progress embodied in new equipment), it means that only new equipment can benefit from the advantage of technological innovations. So, the existing plant will not be able to benefit from its innovations realized during its operating lifetime.[4]

This framework certainly represents a simplification of reality, since it excludes productivity improvements due to labour organization, however possible, while the original plant remains in function. But this simplification allows us to focus on the most relevant aspects of the problems considered, at least for many industrial sectors.

In addition, we will assume that technical progress will only affect labour productivity and the consumption of energy, not considering the productivity increments of the other factors, such as raw materials and services. This will allow us to concentrate the analysis on the most important factors.

In the assumed framework, the firm j that renews the production structure at time $t = 0$, acquiring the new equipment on the market, will sustain an operating cost (that is cost before depreciations) per unit of product $C_j(0)$ that reflects the technical progress embodied until that date. It will be $C_j(0) = C_i(0) = C(0)$, $C_i(t)$ being the operating cost of the most efficient firm i at every t. This operating cost will be lower than the previous cost, according to the intensity of innovation, giving the firm a cost advantage on rivals.

The new operating cost of firm j will be the sum of costs of factors used to produce and sell the product. Precisely:

$$C_j(0) = C_{j,M}(0) + C_{j,L}(0) + C_{j,E}(0) + C_{j,V}(0) + C_{j,A}(0) \tag{4.1}$$

where: $C_{j,M}(0)$ is the cost of raw material; $C_{j,L}(0)$ is the labour cost; $C_{j,E}(0)$ the energy cost; $C_{j,V}(0)$ is the sale cost and $C_{j,A}(0)$ is the administrative cost.

The labour cost per product $C_{j,L}(0)$ depends on the unit price of labour $P_L(0)$ and the technical coefficient, that is the labour quantity needed per unit of product, $K_{jL}(0)$, with respect to the characteristics of the plant structure. It will be:

$$C_{j,L}(0) = P_L(0) \, K_{j,L}(0) \tag{4.2}$$

Therefore, $K_{j,L}(0)$ is the reciprocal of the labour productivity $\Pi_{j,L}(0)$:

$$K_{j,L}(0) = 1/ \Pi_{j,L}(0) \tag{4.3}$$

In a similar way, the cost of energy per product is a function of the unit price of energy $P_E(0)$ and of the technical coefficient, that is the quantity of energy needed per product unit, with respect to the characteristics of the plant structure $K_{j,E}(0)$. It will be:

$$C_{j,E}(0) = P_E(0) \, K_{j,E}(0) \tag{4.4}$$

with $K_{j,E}(0)$ the reciprocal of the energy productivity $\Pi_{j,E}(0)$:

$$K_{j,L}(0) = 1/ \Pi_{j,E}(0)$$

Likewise for raw materials and other materials or services needed to realize the product.

So, the total operating cost of the product $C_j(0)$, for the firm j, will be:

$$C_j(0) = P_M(0)\, K_{j,M}(0) + P_L(0)\, K_{j,L}(0) + P_E(0)\, K_{j,E}(0) + C_{j,V}(0) + C_{j,A}(0) \tag{4.5}$$

where, in addition to the known symbols, $K_{j,M}(0)$ is the technical coefficient of raw materials, and $P_M(0)$ the relative average price, $C_{j,V}(0)$ the sale cost, and $C_{j,A}(0)$ the administrative cost, per unit of product.

The total operating cost of product $C_j(0)$ will reflect the characteristics of the industrial structure of firm j at $t = 0$. But this cost is not constant in time; it will vary in relation to the prices of factors, mainly labour, raw materials and services. This is according to the trend of prices and productivity in the different markets. In addition, the physical aging of production plant, machinery and equipment will cause an increasing number of maintenance and repair hours, and therefore increasing costs per product.

We will assume salaries and prices of raw materials and energy grow over time, according to a yearly constant inflation rate s. In addition, we will assume an increasing number of work hours to be required for maintenance of plant, due to their physical aging, causing the labour cost per product to increase at an annual constant rate r.

With these assumptions, the labour cost per product of the firm j will grow over time, according to the following function:[5]

$$C_{j,L}(t) = P_L(0)\,(1+s)\, K_{j,L}(0)\,(1+r)^t = C_{j,L}(0)\,(1+r+s)^t \tag{4.6}$$

with t = whole years.

We also assume that the administration and sale costs will grow in the same way, at the rate s. Therefore, the operating cost of the product for the firm j will follow a pattern given by:

$$C_j(t) = C_{j,M}(0)(1+s)^t + C_{j,E}(0)(1+s)^t + C_{j,L}(0)(1+r+s)^t$$
$$+ C_{j,V}(0)(1+s)^t + C_{j,A}(0)(1+s)^t \tag{4.7}$$

It will grow in time, according to the value of r and s.

Obviously we could consider different rates of inflation for the various factors, but while this would add complexity to the formal representation, it does not modify the substance of our problem.

Now, consider that the technical progress will affect labour productivity $\Pi_{i,L}$ such that this grows at a yearly constant rate λ_L in the industry, due to the continuous flow of process innovations.

$$\Pi_{i,L}(t) = \Pi_{i,L}(0)(1+\lambda_L)^t \tag{4.8}$$

The most efficient firm, i, that is the one endowed with the most modern plant at each t (year), will benefit from a greater productivity and therefore a lower unit cost of product.[6] The quantity of labour needed for the product will decrease, due to the technical progress, λ_L, according to the relationship:

$$K_{i,L}(t) = \frac{1}{\Pi_{i,L}(0)(1+\lambda_L)^t} = K_{i,L}(0)\frac{1}{(1+\lambda_L)^t} \tag{4.9}$$

Given the price per unit of labour $P_L(0)$, this means the cost of labour per product decreasing at a constant annual rate λ and increasing at a constant rate of inflation s:

$$C_{i,L}(t) = K_{i,L}(0)\frac{1}{(1+\lambda_L)^t}P_L(0)(1+s)^t \tag{4.10}$$

or:

$$C_{i,L}(t) = C_{i,L}(0)\left(\frac{1+s}{1+\lambda_L}\right)^t \tag{4.11}$$

Setting $(1+s)/(1+\lambda_L) = a$, the expression (4.11) becomes:

$$C_{i,L}(t) = C_{i,L}(0)a^t \tag{4.12}$$

This expression clearly shows that the unit cost of labour will decrease when $\lambda_L > s$ $(0 < a < 1)$ and it will grow when $\lambda_L < s$, $(a > 1)$ but at a rate less than s.

If the technical progress also influences energy, causing a productivity increase, the costs of this factor will reduce too. In this way, the unit operating cost of the firm i will follow a pattern given by:

$$C_i(t) = C_{i,M}(0)(1 + s)^t + C_E(0)(1 + s)^t + C_{i,L}(0) a^t +$$

$$C_{i,V}(0)(1 + s)^t + C_{i,A}(0)(1 + s)^t \qquad (4.13)$$

It will increase in time, but at a rate lower than the rate of inflation s. It can also decrease in time, if λ_L is greater than s and the labour cost is the most important component of the product unit cost.

In any case, the technical progress will determine an increasing difference between the costs of the most efficient firms in the market (i) and costs of the firm (j) up until operating with the technical structure set up at $t = 0$ (Figure 4.1).

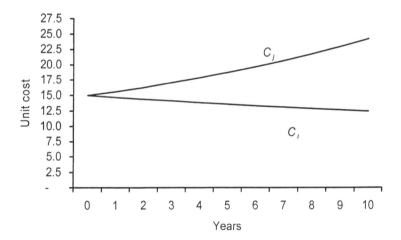

Figure 4.1 *Operating cost difference between the firm* j *and the most efficient firm* i *at each* t *(*$\lambda_L > s$*)*

To be precise, if the other costs remain constant, this difference in costs between firm j and firm i will increase according to the following:

Creating value through innovation

$$C_j(t) - C_i(t) = C_{j,L}(0)(1 + s + r)^t - C_{i,L}(0)a^t \qquad (4.14)$$

If all firms fix their prices using the *full costing method*, that is adding a margin $M(t)$ to operating costs to pay depreciation and yield the invested capital (Dringoli 1980), prices will vary following the operating costs of the most efficient firms $C_i(t)$, according to the following relationship:

$$P(t) = C_i(t) + M(t) \qquad (4.15)$$

We can also assume that the margin $M(t)$ changes according to the inflation rate s and the productivity improvement rate λ_I, in the investment goods industry. As a consequence, the margin $M(t)$ to be added to the operating costs to determine the price of the product will also vary in time and will be precisely:

$$M_i(t) = M_i(0)\left(\frac{1+s}{1+\lambda_I}\right)^t = M_i(0)\, b^{\,t} \qquad (4.16)$$

setting: $b = (1 + s) / (1 + \lambda_I)$.

If $s < \lambda_I$, b will be lower than 1 and therefore the unit margin will decrease over time.

Therefore, in a competitive market, product prices will vary following the operating costs of the most efficient firms, according to the relationship:

$$P(t) = C_i(t) + M(t) = C_M(0)(1 + s)^t + C_{j,V}(0)(1 + s)^t$$

$$+ C_{j,A}(0)(1 + s)^t + C_{i,L}(0)a^t + C_{i,E}(0)(1 + s)^t + M(0)b^{\,t} \qquad (4.17)$$

If $s = 0$, the product prices will have a decreasing trend because of the growth rates of labour productivity. If $0 < s < \lambda$, that is the inflation rate is lower than the growth rate of productivity, prices will increase but at a rate lower than the inflation rate.

In any case, the unit margin $[P(t) - C(t)]$ of the firm j, operating with the production structure set-up at $t = 0$, will decrease over time from positive values to zero and then to negative values. Precisely:

$$P(t) - C_j(t) = C_M(t) + C_V(t) + C_A(0) + C_L(0)a^t + C_E(t) + M(0)b^t$$

$$- C_M(t) - C_E(t) - C_{L,j}(0)(1 + r + s)^t - C_V(t) - C_{j,A}(t) \qquad (4.18)$$

and, simplifying:

$$P(t) - C_j(t) = C_L(0)a^t + M(0)b^t - C_L(0)(1 + r + s)^t \tag{4.19}$$

Therefore, the earnings and cash flow of the firm will decrease in time according to the function illustrated above.

The dynamics of prices and operating expenses of firm *j* are illustrated in Figures 4.2 and 4.3.

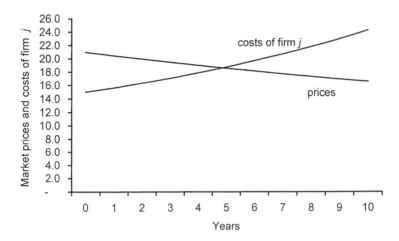

Figure 4.2   Trends of prices and costs of the firm j *if* λ > s

Based on the above functions, the condition for a strategy creating value, for the firm *j*, is as follows:[7]

$$\sum_{t=1}^{T} \{[C_L(0)a^t + M(0)b^t - C_L(0)(1 + r + s)^t] Q(t)(1 - \tau^*)\} / (1 + \rho)^t$$

$$> I(0) \tag{4.20}$$

where:

$$a = \frac{1 + s}{1 + \lambda_L} \; ; \; b = \frac{1 + s}{1 + \lambda_I}$$

The maximum economic life of the equipment (*T*) is determined by solving with respect to *T* the following expression:

$$C_L(0)a^T + M(0)b^T - C_L(0)(1 + r + s)^T = 0 \tag{4.21}$$

Even if the lifetime of production structure T cannot be found by solving the equation, this variable can be determined through simulation.

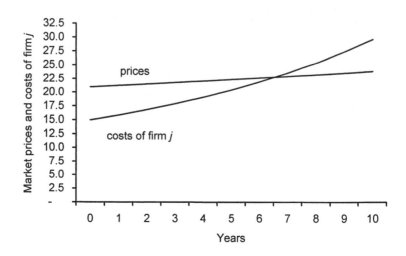

Figure 4.3   Trends of prices and costs of the firm j *if* λ < s

In addition to the known symbols, τ^* is the adjusted tax rate, $Q(t)$ is the programmed sales; T is the lifetime of the technical structure; after this period it stops producing positive cash flows.[8] In particular, the expression (4.20) prescribes that the present value of free cash flows from operations, discounted at the cost of capital ρ (*WACC*), must be greater than the capital invested in the new production structure $I(0)$.[9]

Equation (4.21) prescribes that, in the hypothesis of a residual value of the production structure equal to zero, the lifetime T of the production structure cannot be longer than the period after which the unit cash flow becomes equal to zero from positive values.[10]

The above relations indicate that the value of a process innovation strategy depends on environmental trends, expressed by the parameters r, s, λ_L, λ_E, λ_I, the industry conditions influencing the dynamic of sale prices and the structure of the firm j influencing its operating costs. Among the considered variables, appropriate relationships have to be maintained for the strategy to be capable of creating value, as specified by the model presented above.

A further simplification can be introduced, without relevant differences considering the aim of this analysis, assuming the rate of increase of labour productivity to be the same in the equipment industry and in the industry where the firm being considered operates $(\lambda_i = \lambda_L)$. In this case, the expression (4.21) becomes the following:

$$(C_L(0) + M(0))\left(\frac{1+s}{1+\lambda_L}\right)^T - C_L(0)(1+r+s)^T = 0 \qquad (4.22)$$

$$\frac{C_L(0) + M(0)}{C_L(0)} = \left(\frac{(1+r+s)(1+\lambda_L)}{(1+s)}\right)^T \qquad (4.23)$$

Since the terms $s\lambda_L$ and $r\lambda_L$ are negligible in order of magnitude with respect to the other variables, (4.22) can be simplified into this:

$$\frac{C_L(0) + M(0)}{C_L(0)} = \left(\frac{(1+r+s+\lambda_L)}{(1+s)}\right)^T \qquad (4.24)$$

Expressing (4.24) in logarithms, we can find the variable T. Precisely it will be: [11]

$$T = \frac{\log(C_L(0) + M(0)) - \log C_L(0)}{\log(1+s+r+\lambda_L) - \log(1+s)} \qquad (4.25)$$

With the introduced simplification, the condition for a strategy creating value is:

$$\sum_{t=1}^{T}\left[(C_L(0) + M(0))\left(\frac{1+s}{1+\lambda_L}\right)^t - C_L(0)(1+r+s)^t\right]Q(t)(1-\tau^*)/(1+\rho)^t$$
$$> I(0) \qquad (4.26)$$

The model can be easily extended considering the process innovation will also affect energy and raw material consumption. The energy cost of the most efficient firm i will be, for example:

$$C_{i,E}(t) = C_{i,E}(0)\left(\frac{1+s}{1+\lambda_E}\right)^t \qquad (4.27)$$

where λ_E is the rate of increment of productivity using energy.

THE DRIVING FORCES OF THE STRATEGY VALUE

The model emphasizes that the lifetime of the technical structure (T) is strictly linked to the rate of productivity increase. Once the new technical structure is completed, the firm will obtain positive earnings and cash flows; but during this time competitors will renew their plant or enter the market with more efficient plant, causing a progressive erosion of the margins of firms operating with old equipment.

The model points out the influence of process innovations and technical progress (λ) on the value of the strategy. The higher the rate of productivity increase, the faster the reduction of prices and the shorter the production structure lifetime.

A push to accelerate the changing of the production structure and the introduction of new processes is also given by the decreasing cost of new plant $I(t)$. In this case the obstacle to the immediate and generalized use of new techniques is reduced. On the other hand, when the real investment is more expensive, a rapid adaptation is not convenient and the technical structure of the firm will be largely formed by out-of-date plant.

A great influence on the lifetime of the production structure and on the price trajectory $P(t)$ is also exerted by the ratio between the labour cost and the capital invested per unit of product. The more expensive labour is, compared to capital, the more rapidly the firm will have to adopt the new methods requiring less labour. When labour is cheap, this push fails and the old plant can be kept in use longer. Finally, a higher cost of capital (ρ) requires a longer lifetime of the production structure and higher sales prices.[12]

This model can be generalized in different ways. First, different growth rates of productivity in labour, energy and raw materials and different rates of increment in salary, raw materials prices, energy, etc. can be considered. Second, if the residual value of the technical structure is considered to be different from zero, the total investment could be simply reduced by the discounted residual value.

THE SUSTAINABLE VALUE OF THE FIRM IN THE LONG RUN

In effect, to remain competitive, the firm should have to accomplish a sequence of renewals of the productive structure in the long term.

After it has adopted the new productive structure $I(1)$, other firms will renew their plant, or will enter the market with more efficient plant, triggering the progressive contraction of net cash flows of our firm, according to the relationships already illustrated. In the end, the existing production structure will not provide positive cash flows and the firm will have to make a new investment $I(2)$ and so on, over time (Figure 4.4).

To remain competitive and to preserve value in the long run, a successful firm must realize on time a succession of renewals of technical structure, more or less frequently according to the rate of technical progress in the industry. In theory, the general condition to create value in the long run is given by the general relation (4.28).

$$\sum_{0}^{T1}[FCFO(t)](1-\tau^*)/(1+\rho)^t +$$

$$\sum_{T1}^{T2}[FCFO(t)](1-\tau^*)/(1+\rho)^t +$$

$$.. +$$

$$\sum_{Tn-1}^{Tn}[FCFO(t)](1-\tau^*)/(1+\rho)^t >$$

$$I(0)+I(1)/(1+\rho)^{T1}+I(2)/(1+\rho)^{T2}...+I(n)/(1+\rho)^{Tn} \qquad (4.28)$$

The expression indicates that in the long run the total cash flow, discounted at a ρ rate, must be greater than the total sum of discounted investments, represented by the sequence $I(0)$, $I(1)$, ...$I(n)$.

Thus, in order to keep on creating value, the company will have to sustain the investment sequence required to improve productivity in the long run.

If the company is not capable of producing the necessary cash flows for financing the investments required by technical progress and paying off the invested capital, it must 'leave the scene', to avoid an irreversible process of value disruption. The higher the rate of technical progress λ, the harder it will be for the firm to continue 'playing the game', particularly if the first competitive positioning is weak compared to competitors.

Continuing the 'game' is more difficult when innovation is endogenous and has to be produced inside the same company that will use it. We will focus on this new subject in the section beginning on p. 57.

INDUSTRY STRUCTURE AND PROCESS INNOVATION STRATEGY

The model shown above underlines the importance of prices for the value of strategy. Thus, market conditions in which the firm considered operates are crucial for any strategy to be successful.

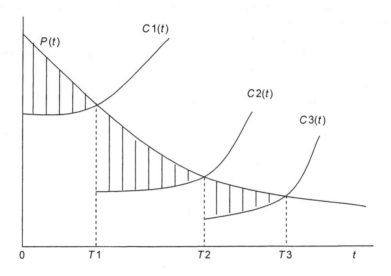

Figure 4.4   The chain of new technical structures

In a perfect competition market (homogeneous products, high number of competitors and no entry barriers), cost reduction, mainly caused by the new techniques, will cause a continuous reduction of product prices. The competitive forces will drive the changes in the firm structure. The decrease in prices will also characterize oligopolistic markets, especially when the new technologies are accessible to competing and potential rivals.

The oligopolistic firms will take advantage of a price reduction policy, to discourage the entry of new firms (Dringoli 1980). Nevertheless product prices will remain well above the prices in perfect competition markets, because of the entry barriers in the sector.

EARLY MOVES AND DELAYS IN STRUCTURAL CHANGES

According to our model, a firm will change its production structure when cash flow becomes zero.

On one hand, the process innovation can be introduced in advance, if it gives significant advantages over competitors. On the other hand, it can be delayed when new and more effective improvements in production techniques are on the way (Adams and Dirlam 1966).

The expectation for a relevant technological change may cause not only a delay in the adoption of the new techniques, but it may also influence the features of the selected innovations. The firm can decide, for example, to choose cheaper solutions for its plant, waiting for the introduction of a more radical new technology (Rosemberg 1976).

In other cases, if a radical technological innovation can break the industry equilibrium, giving the first mover relevant advantages, it may be better to anticipate the change of the firm structure.

Quickly realizing innovations can be crucial for gaining a strong competitive advantage and/or preventing any competitors' moves. Being the first innovator may imply becoming the leader in technical innovation and assuming control of the competitors' growth, through a patent system or other means.

Finally, when structural changes produce relevant cost reductions, it can be an advantage for the firm to start a price war against its competitors, to drive them out of the market. In this case, there is a premium for the first user of new techniques, so that the most dynamic firm will create new productive capacity, determining the transformation of the industry structure.

THE VALUE OF A PROCESS INNOVATION STRATEGY: A SIMULATION

To clarify the influence of different variables, we will illustrate an application of the model just presented. The data used for calculating the value of the strategy are shown in Table 4.1.

We suppose environmental trends are characterized by different rates of labour productivity increase in the industry (λ_L): case A = 7%; case B = 4%; case C = 2%.

In hypothesis A, the value of the innovation strategy is negative and approximately equal to −7 million euro; the lifetime of the new equipment is around 4 years.

In hypothesis B, the value of the strategy results as being positive and equal to 25 million euro, with an economic lifetime of the new equipment of 7 years (Figure 4.5). In hypothesis C, the value of the strategy reaches 70 million euro and the economic lifetime of the new equipment is 8 years (Table 4.1).

In hypothesis A, the environmental trends are characterized by a rate of technical progress equal to 7% and the firm is not capable of creating value and must leave the industry. To successfully run the business, it is necessary to change some strategy features, for example saving in investment or increasing the quantities sold, etc.

Table 4.1   The value of a process innovation strategy: simulation data

	Case A	Case B	Case C
Growth rate of costs due to the deterioration of the production structure (r)	0.05	0.05	0.05
Growth rate of costs due to inflation (s)	0.03	0.03	0.03
Average growth rate of product unit cost ($s + r$)	0.08	0.08	0.08
Average growth rate of labour productivity (λ_L)	0.07	0.04	0.02
Cost of capital (*WACC*)	0.1	0.1	0.1
Adjusted tax rate τ^*	0.25	0.25	0.25
$C_L(0)$ in €	8	8	8
$M(0)$ in €	6	6	6
$C_M(0) + C_E(0) + C_V(0) + C_A(0)$	7.00	7.00	7.00
Unit production cost $C(0)$, in €	15	15	15
Sales (quantities in million sq.m)	10	10	10
$P(0)$ in €	21	21	21
Investment in € million	100	100	100
Value of the strategy (€ million)	−25.0	5.5	34.5
Duration T (years)	5	6	8

Source: Author's elaboration.

In order to illustrate the different influence of the variables considered, we have also calculated the value of the strategy under different hypotheses regarding the initial price $P(0)$ and the cost of capital ρ. The results obtained from these simulations provide the following indication.

The higher the annual rate of the technical progress λ, and so the faster the expected reduction of sale prices, the higher the initial margin will have to be, as will the price, since its reduction over time is quicker and therefore the plant lifetime period will be shorter.

The higher the discount rate ρ, the higher the initial gross margin will have to be, as will the sale prices.

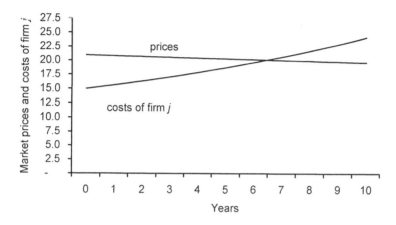

Figure 4.5   Prices and costs dynamics: a simulation (case B)

PRODUCTIVITY IMPROVEMENT STRATEGIES THROUGH ENDOGENOUS INNOVATION

In the previous sections we considered technical progress as an exogenous variable for the firm. This is a suitable point of view for sectors in which firms play a minor role in innovation of production processes, compared to innovation achieved by producers of plant and equipment.

Differently, in this section we assume that a firm operates in a sector where technical progress is not produced outside, but is mainly created inside the firms (endogenous technical progress).[13] For competing successfully, a firm has to organize and implement R&D activities suitable for creating technical innovations (new machinery, new processes and so on) capable of improving the productivity of inputs used.[14] We refer to firms big enough to develop their own R&D activity.

There are many examples of innovative firms operating in steel, chemical, oil refining and other sectors that created innovations through internal R&D activities (see Strategy Focus at the end of this chapter). In recent times, a relevant flow of innovations has concerned other sectors, as shown by data concerning productivity provided by the United States Department of Labor. On this topic, see Table 3.2.

When technical progress is endogenous, a firm will have to set challenging objectives in terms of productivity, in order to strengthen its competitive position. But these objectives must be compatible with the available resources. The more challenging the objectives, the higher the investments in R&D will be to fulfil them, and the higher the probability of R&D failures. This is true because the research activity will become more unpredictable, having to pursue knowledge farther away from present technologies. For this reason, a firm must pursue viable research objectives, since R&D success is highly correlated to a clear definition of objectives and such a definition is more difficult when research deals with unexplored fields.

The analysis of conditions making innovation strategies profitable goes along the lines described in previous sections, with the very relevant difference that, in the case of endogenous progress, there are extra variables influencing the innovation strategy, namely the R&D investments needed to achieve the planned rate of innovation.

A MODEL FOR EVALUATING ENDOGENOUS PROCESS INNOVATIONS

In order to define an innovation strategy creating value, we have to consider that, after the production structure is changed, prices will decline according to the rate of productivity improvement in the sector (λ_L). While the product price will decrease at a rate λ_L, the operating costs of our firm will grow because of the rate of inflation s and the rate of equipment deterioration r.

The condition for the innovation strategy creating value is the following:

$$\sum_{t=1}^{T} [C_L(0)a^t + M(0)^t - C_L(0)(1 + r + s)^t]\, Q(t)\, (1 - \tau)\, /\, (1 + \rho)^t$$

$$\geq I(0) + I_{R\&S}(0) \qquad\qquad (4.29)$$

where:

$$a = \frac{1+s}{1+\lambda_L}\, ; b = \frac{1+s}{1+\lambda_I}$$

and the new term $I_{R\&D}$ represents the investment in R&D activities.

The maximum economic life of the equipment (T) is determined by solving the following expression with respect to T:

$$C_L(0)a^T + M(0)b^T = C_{j,L}(1 + r + s)^T \qquad (4.30)$$

The conclusions just drawn in the case of exogenous technical progress can be extended to endogenous process innovations. In addition we point out that the firm will have lower labour costs than rivals, if the R&D activities are successful in determining labour productivity improvement higher than the average in the sector. Thus it will be able to increase its competitive advantage and value by a chain of successful structural changes.

INDUSTRY STRUCTURE AND TECHNOLOGICAL INNOVATIONS

Industry structure can limit a firm's development, because of the influence on product prices and margin levels and thus on the amount of resources available for structural changes.

According to various authors, competitive oligopoly is the market structure that can promote most innovations. On one hand the reduced number of competitors and their dimension allows for higher earnings and thus higher investments in R&D; on the other hand competition between oligopolistic firms creates the adequate pressure for innovations to be pursued and put on the market as soon as possible.

In order for this to happen, it is necessary that oligopolistic firms are not allowed to organize trusts, in order to exploit productive structures for the longest time possible. On this subject the agreement between Standard Oil of Indiana and G. Farben is emblematic for delaying the development of synthetic rubber in the USA, before the war. Another case is represented by the agreement between DuPont and ICI for dividing world markets between themselves and reducing competition.

However, if technological innovation is influenced by industry structure, the industry structure itself can be deeply transformed by the introduction of innovations by the most dynamic firms. This has happened in many industrial sectors, where technological progress favoured the concentration of industry, through the exclusion from the market of small and medium-sized firms (Phillips 1971). Examples of significant innovations in productive processes that deeply transformed industry structure took place in the steel industry as well as in the paper, chemical, refining and a number of other industries.

It must also be noted that, for creating advantages by attacking competitors' market shares, it is necessary that cost advantages are relevant and rather strong so as to protect the firm from possible retaliations. Only under such conditions does an innovative firm have an advantage in reducing its prices and expanding its products, thereby damaging its rivals.

For reaching such an objective, the innovative firm may find it useful to adopt elimination prices, in order to accelerate the exit of inefficient firms from the market. To obtain such a result in the short run, prices will have to be set at a level lower than the operative cost of the firms to be eliminated. Conversely, if this objective has to be reached in the long run, the leader will only have to set prices equal to operative costs, reducing them at a rate equal to the rate of planned and achieved productivity increment (λ_P).

Favourable conditions for a policy of elimination prices are given by an industry structure where there are a few big players and a number of smaller firms, operating at higher unit costs. The possibility for obtaining high productivity increments using high dimension plant (scale economies) will also push the firm into adopting a policy of elimination prices.

Obviously, such a strategy must be carefully evaluated. The costs of such a strategy are due to lower current cash flows caused by the competitors' reaction. The advantages are given by the higher cash flows the firm can achieve, after the elimination of some competitors and the acquisition of a higher position in the sector, giving power over prices.

SCALE ECONOMIES AND PROCESS INNOVATION STRATEGIES

Sometimes technical progress results in the construction of new plant with a high increase in the scale of production.

Numerous examples can be found in the chemical and cement industries, as well as in steel and in non-iron-related metallurgy. In general, relevant scale economies appear in sectors where production is continuous and automatically regulated and employs robotics (Freeman 1968; Hughes 1971; Pratten 1971; Gold 1976; Grant 1998).

Every time technical progress results in new plant involving a large increase in production scale, the change of production structure creates an expansion of the productive capacity of the firm making the investment. Thus, the direct consequence of the innovation strategy is a net increase in supply and the consequent fall of product prices, if demand does not grow appropriately.

These effects reduce the cash flow of the firm up to the point of shutting down the most obsolete plant, boosted by the price reduction, and do not bring back supply to the starting point of equilibrium. The sector will experience a reduction in the number of working plants and a reallocation of market shares, benefiting the firm that first made this transformation.

In these circumstances, it is also possible that competitors build new plant, expanding total productive capacity in advance of their schedule. In this case the excess of supply becomes structural and can produce dramatic consequences on prices and cash flows for all firms.

Such a situation only ends when an expansion of demand absorbs the structural supply excess.

If demand does not increase, the industry can experience an excess in production capacity, with prices going below average costs. Under these conditions, less efficient firms, with operating costs higher than market prices, will shut down, favouring the growth of the most dynamic firms and the concentration of industry.

For these reasons, any decision regarding the expansion of productive capacity must be accurately weighted as to the risks. Two issues are of particular relevance: future demand and competitors' behaviour.

A favourable condition for the expansion of productive capacity is a high elasticity of demand. In this case demand will absorb the extra production and the firm will have an advantage in renewing and expanding its technical structure. On the other hand, when the growth of demand is not high, situations characterized by capacity excess and consequent price reduction may occur.

To avoid such situations, a leading firm will discourage competitors from increasing production capacity, using deterrents such as:

- clearly signalling a programme of relevant increment in production capacity;
- operating to get a larger market share and competing aggressively in order to force competitors out of the market;
- buying competitors' plant;
- reducing the exit costs of rivals in the industry;
- expressing pessimistic forecasts on the evolution of the demand, so as to discourage competitors.

Obviously, a market leader will enjoy a privileged position from which it can put such manoeuvres into action. Under these conditions, some new plants can be built in addition to the existing ones and not only in substitution of them, in order to gain market share and a greater bargaining capacity in determining prices. At the same time, this decision will allow the firm to gain a stronger capacity for controlling the introduction of new technologies.

However, an aggressive production and market share expansion strategy is really risky, especially when the discontinuities in technologies make the market space left by minor firms insufficient.

High demand elasticity on prices creates, instead, favourable conditions for such a strategy; in these conditions price reduction becomes a compelling factor in the process of industrial concentration and the advantage of the expansion strategy is no longer closely linked to the industry structure.

There are no substantial changes in the analytical conditions under which the strategy of productivity improvement creates value. Regarding the model previously described, it is also a matter of considering the increase of production $Q(t)$.

PROCESS INNOVATIONS AND SUSTAINABLE COMPETITIVE ADVANTAGE

For creating value in sectors characterized by continuous process innovations, firms must plan and implement technological innovation and carry out the consequent changes in their technical structure.

If the firm cannot sustain the R&D expenses necessary for maintaining a rate of productivity increment at least equal to the average rate of increment of productivity in the sector (λ_L^*), because of either the insufficient dimension or the scarce innovative capacity of its resources, it will have to leave the sector to enter other markets, where it can perform better, given its resources and competences.

Conversely, a firm capable of maintaining increments in labour productivity higher than those of its competitors will get higher cash flows. These will allow the firm to channel larger amounts of resources to its R&D activities, further increasing the superiority gap over its rivals.

Since process technologies are the core of competitive advantage in a number of industries, it is crucial that the firm's top management know these technologies well enough in order to understand and quickly apply them. This brings the focus back on the importance of the non-material components of the firm's structure, that is the technological and managerial know-how, largely not codified and deriving from individual skills and learning-by-doing processes.

In order to underline the crucial importance of process innovations in international competition, Thurow (1992) argued that usually the top managers of American firms were on average less prepared from a technological point of view than their European and Japanese colleagues.

According to the author, only 30% of the top managers in the US had a technological background compared to 70% of European and Japanese managers and this difference in knowledge had caused American firms to be slower in adapting new process technologies such as flexible workstations, just-in-time handling of the warehouse and the statistical control of quality. Thurow cites, as an example, the case of the American steel industry, 20 years ago, where the new technology of continuous casting kilns was adopted after a delay of 6–7 years with respect to European and Japanese competitors, because the managers did not understand the technological revolution under way and were reluctant to take risks. This delay by the American firms caused a big erosion in their market share and profits.

STRATEGY FOCUS: PRODUCTIVITY TRENDS AND PROCESS INNOVATIONS IN SOME RELEVANT INDUSTRIES

Productivity Trends and Process Innovations in the Italian Ceramic Tile Industry

When analysing the productivity trends in the Italian ceramic tile industry, the importance of process innovation for firm competitiveness clearly stands out.

Data regarding labour productivity and unit consumption of heat energy in the Italian ceramic tile industry from 1973 to 1991 are shown in Table 4.2, Figure 4.6 and Figure 4.7. They are the consequence of some important technological innovations that characterized this sector: the roll kiln for once-fired tiles, the plant mechanizing charge and discharge operations from the kiln and the plant mechanizing glazing operations.

In particular, the introduction of the roll kiln at the end of the 1970s made it possible to reduce fuel, because of the elimination of a large quantity of fettling. The theoretic consumption of energy passed from 2100/1500 Kcal/Kg in a tunnel kiln to 550/300 Kcal/Kg in a roll kiln!

But the most important effect was the reduction of time for tile cooking, by virtue of putting tiles in only one layer running on rolls of special steel. The single layer kiln introduced at the end of the 1970s permitted a reduction in the cooking time from 16 hours, with the tunnel kiln, to approximately one hour (55 min).

At the beginning the roll kiln required a larger number of employees than the tunnel kiln with trucks, but some years later these operations were also mechanized.

The introduction of the single layer kiln brought about the modification of the charge and discharge plant as well as the glazing line. New plant for the automation of glazing lines was introduced later, using a microprocessor in systems for moving products. In subsequent years the use of microprocessors spread to other phases of the production process.

Table 4.2 Labour productivity and heat energy consumption in the Italian ceramic tile industry

Year	New plant	Labour productivity sq. m year/ employee	Unit consumption heat energy methane: cm/sq. m
1971		4,939	4.787
1972		5,192	4.989
1973	Tunnel oven	5,245	4.679
1974		4,936	5.139
1975		4,870	5.932
1976		5,080	5.148
1977	Roll oven single firing	5,768	5.424
1978		6,209	5.120
1979		6,739	5.031
1980	Roll oven single firing: diffusion	7,204	4.818
1981	Mechanization of charge and discharge operations	7,674	4.870
1982		7,870	4.557
1983		8,026	4.365
1984		9,720	3.916
1985		9,842	3.595
1986	Mechanization of glazing operations	11,229	3.410
1987		12,069	3.314
1988		12,747	2.824
1989		14,230	2.841
1990		14,186	2.562
1991		14,018	2.502

Source: Author's elaboration on Società Ceramica Italiana data, 1971–1991.

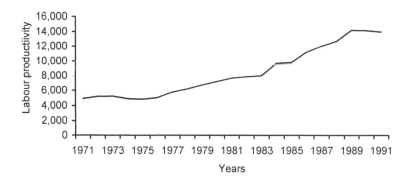

Source: Author's elaboration on Società Ceramica Italiana data, 1971–1992.

Figure 4.6 Labour productivity (annual sq. metres per employee) in the Italian ceramic tile industry

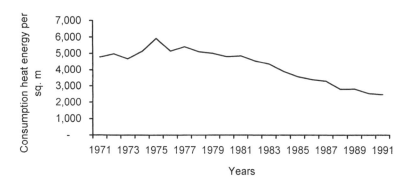

Source: Author's elaboration on Società Ceramica Italiana data, 1971–1992.

Figure 4.7 Heat energy consumption in the Italian ceramic tile industry

The roll kiln, introduced initially for the production of *monocottura* (single-fired) tiles, spread also to *bicottura* tiles (twice-fired tiles).

In addition to these radical innovations, many incremental innovations spread in the sector, continuously reducing heat energy consumption and improving labour productivity up until the present day. Other incremental innovations were realized in raw materials for glazes with a consequent reduction in prices of raw materials and packaging (Figure 4.8).

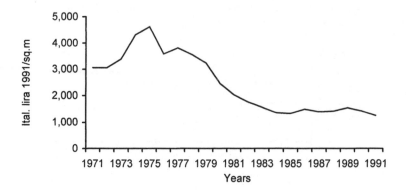

Source: Author's elaboration on Società Ceramica Italiana data, 1971–1992.

Figure 4.8   Cost of raw materials for glazes in the Italian ceramic tile
industry

Despite a continuous improvement of the product in its technical and aesthetic values, the overall effect was a continuous decline in the production cost of tiles, as shown in Figure 4.9.

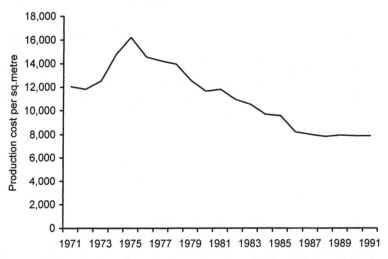

Source: Author's elaboration on Società Ceramica Italiana data, 1971–1992.

Figure 4.9   Dynamics of production costs in the Italian ceramic tile industry
(1971–1991)

Also product prices, especially after 1977, declined, confirming the strong competitive pressure in the industry (Figure 4.10).

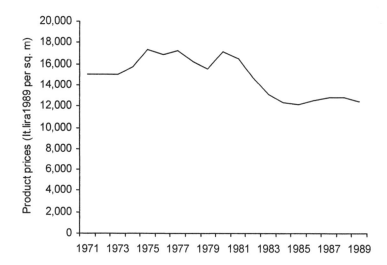

Source: Author's elaboration on Società Ceramica Italiana data, 1971–1992.

Figure 4.10   *Dynamics of sale prices in the Italian ceramic tile industry (1971–1989)*

As a consequence of the increasing competition by innovation, the number of ceramic firms operating in Italy decreased from 465 in 1974 to 352 in 1988 and 207 in 2006. The workforce decreased from 44,823 employees in 1974 to 40,708 in 1982 and to 28,093 at the end of 2006.

At the end of 2006 the Italian ceramic industry reported a total turnover of €5,742 million with a production of 568 million square metres.

The overall production had been 230 million square metres in 1974 and 323 million in 1982.

The Process Innovation Strategy of the Marazzi Group

Marazzi installed the first rapid single firing roll kiln (monocottura) in one of its factories with the collaboration of SITI.

The innovation, patented in 1974, was introduced by Marazzi in 1977 and later adopted by other Italian firms that bought the production technology and the necessary glazes. Soon after other firms undertook the production of kilns and machinery for production of monocottura tiles. This was a real technological breakthrough with the reduction of the production cycle duration from 3–4 days to the current 3–4 hours.

Marazzi expanded its business considerably, both by acquisition and direct investment. Today Marazzi is a leading tile-producing company and has operations in Spain, France, Russia and the USA, in addition to those in Italy.

In 2004 the Group recorded €777 million revenues and produced 83 million square metres of ceramic tiles.

In 2006 the Group reached $964 million revenues and $180 million *EBITDA* with a workforce of around 6300 people in 19 production plants and reached 14,500 sale units in more than 130 countries. It produces both white and red-body interior and exterior floor tiles in different formats and designs. The reference market is the global market; at the end of 2006 approximately 70% of sales were obtained outside Italy (Marazzi, Annual Report, 2004, 2005, 2006).

Note that in 2006 the average size of Italian ceramic tile companies was 135 employees (Società Ceramica Italiana, annual report 2006).

Ever since its origin, the Group has dedicated important resources to R&D, producing the technology needed to realize its products either in-house or in collaboration with the principal plant and machinery manufacturers.

The development of important technological know-how internal to the Group has allowed the Group to obtain a competitive advantage over competitors.

In 1985 the Group introduced and patented the innovative process 'Firestream'; this process, carrying out the glazing on an incandescent stand, makes it possible to produce tiles characterized by high resistance and aesthetic uniformity, particularly suitable to applications in industrial and commercial sectors.

The R&D direction also participates in process development projects together with the most important producers of technological innovation (Sacmi, System Tecnitalia, Nuova Firma and SIL). In addition the Group collaborates with universities and research institutes on the development of new processes and new technologies.

In 2006 the R&D expenses reached €5.3 million. Most of all the internal R&D activity on production process generates non-patented know-how, such as formulas for slurry and solutions for tuning-up processes.

Process Innovations and Productivity Improvements in the Steel Industry

Another significant example of the effects of technical progress incorporated in new plant and machinery with regard to competition is offered by innovations in the steel sector.[15]

The sector is characterized by important labour productivity improvements stemming from a sequence of innovations in kilns and fusion processes, from automation of charge and discharge operations, process control, improvements in the stocking and enrichment of the combustion, extension of the life of fettlings and reduction of scraps.

On this subject, see the data shown in Figure 4.11 on the productivity improvements in the steel industry from 1904 to 1970.

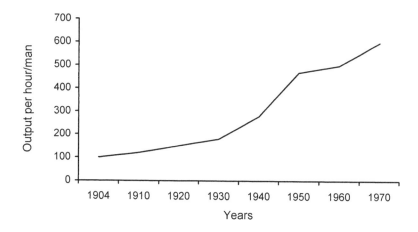

Source: Gold (1976).

*Figure 4.11   Productivity improvements in the steel industry: physical output
per man-hour (1904 = 100)*

The introduction of new technologies and improved labour skills has increased labour productivity further in recent years. Over the period 1983–1993 labour productivity of the major integrated steel makers grew at an annual compound rate of between 5.6% and 9.5% (Demura 1995; Paine Webber 1995).

On this subject see data shown in Figures 4.12 and 4.13. They clearly explain the success on the world markets of the Chinese, Japanese and Korean firms together with the Australian BHP.

The importance of process innovations, for creating value in this industry, remains unchanged today, both in the large enterprises operating in the mass market and in medium enterprises operating in different market segments with special products.

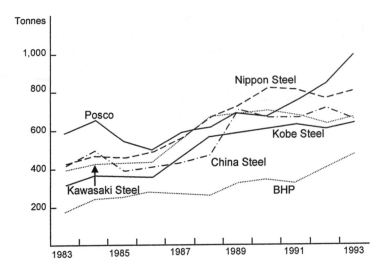

Source: Paine Webber (1995).

Figure 4.12 Productivity improvements in the steel industry: physical output (annual tonnes) per employee

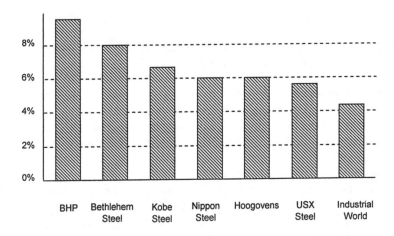

Source: Paine Webber (1995).

Figure 4.13 Productivity growth in the steel industry (annual compound growth rate 1983–1993)

A recent interview released to *La Repubblica* (2006) by Giovanni Arvedi, owner of the successful homonymous firm, specialized in steel production, is particularly enlightening.

> I believe in steel and innovation; within 2008, thanks to the collaboration with Siemens, a new plant, even more productive than the previous one, will come to birth in Cremona. It is an investment of 300 million euros to build the first plant in the world able to directly produce in continuous hot rolled coils, starting from liquid steel. Thanks to 20 patents of Arvedi, the new plant with ESP (Endless Strip Production) technology will be only 170 metres long, instead of the two kilometres of a traditional factory. But it is not all, since ESP, in addition to skipping a whole production phase, that of cold lamination, will enable the production of very subtle coils (I'm saying that we want to reach 0.9 and 0.8 millimetres and perhaps 0.7 and 0.6 millimetres). Therefore, the quality to provide better products to producers of cars, appliances, and to the aeronautic industry. But it will also enable a technological breakthrough the industry has not witnessed for decades. It is confirmed by the robust cost reduction for the start-up of the plant (−30%) and the strong drop in energy expenses. ESP will enable a cut in energy consumption of 75%, and since energy is the highest cost the metallurgy of iron has to sustain, higher than raw material, it is a very important advantage. (p. 12)

Arvedi Group is a medium-sized firm located in Lombardy (Italy) specializing in production, transformation and distribution of flat rolled carbon steel products, carbon steel tubes, stainless steel tubes and thin gauge stainless steel strip.

The above mentioned innovative plant has been completed and is Europe's first and the world's second mini-mill for flat rolled steel production. The new production process, based on the innovative ISP (Inline Strip Production) technology allows the liquid steel from the melt shop to be transformed into best quality ultra-thin gauge hot rolled coils in a single and extremely compact cycle.

The strategy of the company, aimed at high quality production and at cost reduction through investments in innovative and avant-garde technologies, has allowed the company to acquire a solid position in the market and to obtain an excellent performance. In the period 2004–2007 the investments have increased from 33.5 million to 149.3 million with an improvement of the labour productivity equal to 29%; in this period the turnover has increased by 43.4%, the EBITDA by 51% and the ROI has passed from 17.6% to 25.4 % (Table 4.3).

According to the company's CEO the strategy for the future aims, on one hand, at the growth into the core business and, on the other, at the commercial exploitation of Arvedi ISP ESP technology in the international market for steel-making plants.

Table 4.3   Arvedi Group's main figures

	2004	2005	2006	2007
Consolidated turnover (€/million)	943.0	995.0	1,160.0	1,353.0
Turnover per employee (€/000)	588.0	621.0	718.0	759.0
EBITDA (€/million)	111.2	108.8	133.6	168.5
Investments (€/million)	33.5	39.2	68.7	149.3
EBITDA/ turnover (%)	11.8	10.9	11.5	12.4
ROE Net income/net worth (%)	23.1	9.7(*)	15.9	20.9
ROI Operating profit/net invested capital (%)	17.6	14.9(*)	23.9	25.4

Note: (*) The drop in the values is mainly due to the revaluation of assets as provided by the 2006 Finance Act.

Source: www. arvedi.it

Process Innovations, Scale Economies and Productivity Improvements in the Chemical Industry

Interesting cases of process innovations also involving scale economies can be found in the steel, chemical, paper and oil and gas industries. In the Table 4.4 is shown the evolution of the typical (efficient) production scale for the most important chemical products in Europe, over the period 1955–1970.

The rapid technical progress and scale economies were the main cause of the progressive deterioration of prices that affected a number of chemical products. Among them we cite ethylene, sterol and butadiene, as shown by various empirical researches (Table 4.5).

Table 4.4 *Growth of typical scale of production of European plant for the most important chemical products*

	1955		1960		1965		1970	
	Tons per year	Index	Tons per year	Index	Tons per year	Index	Tons per year	Index
Aceltaid	10,000	1.0	20,000	2.0	30,000	3.0	100,000	10.0
Acrylonitrile	10,000	1.0	15,000	1.5	30,000	3.0	60,000	6.0
Ammoniac	50,000	1.0	85,000	1.7	150,000	3.0	350,000	7.0
Chlorox	25,000	1.0	50,000	2.0	70,000	2.8	100,000	5.0
Vinyl chloride monomer	30,000	1.0	50,000	1.7	100,000	3.3	150,000	4.0
Ethylene	20,000	1.0	50,000	2.5	150,000	7.5	300,000	15.0
Phenol	10,000	1.0	25,000	2.5	45,000	4.5	70,000	7.0
Ethylene oxide	5,000	1.0	10,000	2.0	20,000	4.0	70,000	14.0
Polyethylene high density	5,000	1.0	10,000	2.0	20,000	4.0	60,000	12.0
Polyethylene low density	10,000	1.0	30,000	3.0	50,000	5.0	200,000	20.0
Sterol	10,000	1.0	30,000	3.0	50,000	5.0	150,000	15.0
Urea	30,000	1.0	80,000	2.7	150,000	5.0	300,000	10.0

Source: Mediobanca R&S (1970 p. 64).

Creating value through innovation

Table 4.5   Price variation of some chemical products in the period
1964–1974 (current and real prices)

Product	Prices in US cents per pound	1964	1974	Change % 1964–1974
Benzene	current	3.40	3.67	+8
	real	3.40	2.57	−24
Butadiene	current	11.75	10.75	−9
	real	11.75	7.52	−36
Ethylene	current	5.06	3.38	−35
	real	5.06	2.34	−54
Sterol	current	12.46	7.50	−40
	real	12.46	5.24	−58
Toluene	current	2.90	3.56	+23
	real	2.90	2.49	−14

Source: De La Mare (1977).

NOTES

1. We will use the term 'plant' or 'machine' when referring to machinery and technical equipment, etc. as a whole which characterize the technical structure of the firm.
2. Industries such as electronics, microwaves, integrated circuits, digital watches, and computers had to face strong tensions on prices, with yearly decreases equal to 29% in the first half of the 1980s. See Williamson (1992, p. 6).
3. In the framework described, at each instant, in the industry, plant built at different times will be in function, incorporating the best techniques of the time in which it was installed. On this subject see Salter (1966).
4. The adopted approach refers to the so-called *vintage capital model*; the fundamentals of this model consist in the fact that the capital is not considered a homogeneous stock, but a series of stratifications of past investments, each of them having specific characteristics and

representing a more efficient technology than the previous one. While in the case of disembodied technical progress all the existing machines are instantaneously reforged with the introduction of a new technique, in the vintage model this operation concerns only the new equipment, that is the new series added to the operating whole, while the older capital section, having become obsolete, is eliminated. In this way the remaining structure is unchanged, according to the age of the capital. The empirical implications of this model are that each industry will use more than one technology at each instant of time. On this subject, see the pioneering contributions of Solow (1960) and Salter (1966). A review of the vintage framework is in Amendola (1976).

5. To be precise it would be $C_j(t) = C_j(0)(1 + r + s + rs)^t$, but the rs term can be eliminated being of insignificant value. Note that, instead of continuous functions, a discrete formulation has been assumed, using the usual measurements in annual jumps. The discrete form has been also used in the simulations presented in this book as being likely to accord more closely with business practice.

6. At each t the most technologically advanced firm is the one that has renewed at the time t and so this firm will always be different. We will indicate it, for simplicity, with the symbol i, which does not identify a specific firm, but the generic firm that at each t is the most technologically advanced.

7. Financial literature generally agrees in considering the net discounted value as the best method to evaluate investments. On this subject see: Brealey and Meyers (1996); Bierman and Smidt (1984); Levy and Sarnat (1986).

8. As seen in Chapter 1, τ^* is the fiscal rate on incomes revised in order to consider the fiscal benefits on depreciations.

9. The expression in brackets can be considered, with reasonable approximation, equivalent to the free cash flow from operations of the firm j. The difference is given by the variation of the net working capital; in the considered framework (absence of growth), we can assume this variation equal to zero.

10. This simplification can be accepted in practice, because much industrial equipment commonly has little, if any, salvage value. In addition, time discount makes this value, at the time of the investment decision, insignificant. However, in the cases where the ultimate scrap value of the equipment is expected to be significantly high, a simple approximation can be used. The approximation is to subtract the future estimated scrap value from its value when installed.

11. Expressing (4.24) in logarithms with base $\alpha = (1 + r + s + \lambda_L)/(1 + s)$, we obtain an equivalent equation that permits obtaining the variable T as:

$$T = \log_\alpha [C(0) + M(0))/C(0)] = \log_\alpha e \log[(C(0) + M(0))/C(0)] =$$

$$= \frac{\log \dfrac{C_L(0) + M(0)}{C(0)}}{\log \alpha} = \frac{\log(C_L(0) + M(0)) - \log C_L(0)}{\log(1 + r + s + \lambda) - \log(1 + s)}$$

12. The actualization rate ρ indicates the opportunity cost of capital and therefore it is a function of the risk of the investment. For an in-depth analysis see: Brealey and Myers (1996); Bierman and Smidt (1984); Levy and Sarnat (1986); Copeland and Weston (1988).

13. It is common knowledge that in modern industrial environments, new technologies no longer derive from the production activity itself, but rather from research centres, in particular those that are located inside the firms. See: Freeman (1974); Amendola (1976).

14. 'Research' means original investigation aimed at the discovery of new scientific knowledge and 'development' represents the technical activity regarding all the problems to overcome and to put into practice the scientific knowledge acquired. In other words *research* is directed at acquiring new knowledge, *development* is directed at creating

applications for the new knowledge, through experiments, prototype development and the planning of new plant.

15. On this subject see also Clark (1987).

5. Creating value through product innovation strategies

INTRODUCTION AND OBJECTIVES

Many industries are characterized by a continuous flow of product innovations, due to technical progress and change in consumer behavioural patterns.

In these dynamic environments the capability to create value depends on systematic product innovation. This is the strategy adopted by many successful companies, such as Sony, Intel, Microsoft, etc. In these environments a firm which does not succeed in keeping pace with its competitors does not survive. Despite the uncertainty of results, the firm must accept the game of innovation, if it wants to survive in these markets.

To create value the entrepreneur has to plan the introduction of product innovations and the change of firm structure.

In this chapter we analyse the most relevant variables for the innovation strategy and the fundamental relationships among them. In addition a quantitative model will be proposed to identify the conditions for a sustainable value of the firm.

ENVIRONMENT TRENDS AND PRODUCT INNOVATIONS

In many industries product innovations represent the most relevant changes influencing the firm's performance. They can be determined both by technical progress and by change in customers' needs and requests. In some cases product innovations go hand in hand with process innovations, as in the high technology sectors (information technology, software, pharmaceutical, microprocessor, etc.). In other cases process innovations are less significant and can be overlooked, as in the clothing industry, footwear, food, etc.

Product innovations can be represented by new types or models of a basic product (new models of cars, software, etc.) or by new basic products (new chemical entities, new electronic products (such as DVDs, mobile phones, HD Tel, etc.).

Whether the innovations are incremental or radical, they will cause a progressive reduction in the sales of old products. Thus, the firm must plan the renewal of old products to avoid the decline of its market share and the consequent reduction of firm value.

To make this possible, it is necessary for the firm to organize a methodical exploration of opportunities offered by applied research and to develop systematic R&D activities. With the introduction of the new product, a new research line has to be planned, so that another generation of products can be launched when the sales of old products start falling.

To obtain success in the long run, a firm periodically has to restore competitive advantage through a systematic innovation of products.

We have many examples of this strategy among leading firms operating in the high technology sectors, such as Apple (with its iPod radical innovation), 3M (€1 billion per year in new products and materials investments), Nokia (€4 billion per year in R&D).

But this strategy is also largely adopted by companies operating in mass markets, with lower technology products, such as Johnson & Johnson (30% of its products with a lifetime of less than three years) and L'Oréal (more than ten new products and models launched every year on the market).

THE VALUE OF A PRODUCT INNOVATION STRATEGY: RELEVANT VARIABLES

To estimate the value of a strategy of product innovation, it is necessary to consider:

1. the investment in R&D activity and in new production capacity;
2. the dynamics of sales and costs of the new product;
3. the cost of capital.

With regard to sales of a new product, generally they show dynamics characterized by four different phases (or stages): introduction, growth, maturity and decline (Levitt 1963a; Kotler 1990; Lambin 1996).

In the *introduction stage* sales are low and the rate of market penetration is slow because the product is not widely known, customers lack experience of the product and there are difficulties in organizing its physical distribution. The *growth stage* is characterized by accelerating market penetration as products meet customer preferences; the product technology becomes more standardized and prices fall. The new buyers stimulate others who are in contact with them, for social and economic reasons, so that a chain reaction develops, determining a rapid diffusion of the product and increasing sales.

The onset of the *maturity stage* is caused by the increase of sales to a level of saturation; once this level is reached, demand is wholly for replacement. Finally the product is challenged by technologically superior substitute products launched by rival firms and it enters its *decline stage* (Figure 5.1).

The duration of the life cycle and of the different stages differs from one product to another, depending on the intensity of innovation and the characteristics of the social and economic environment.

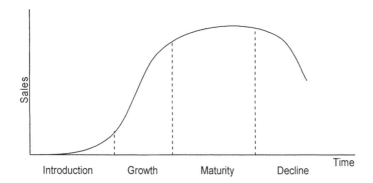

Figure 5.1   Classical life cycle of a new product

In the case where the firm introduces a new type or model of a basic product, the four life-phases generally have a short duration. In particular, the introduction stage can be strongly reduced by already affirmed relationships between firm and customers, due to well known products or well known and appreciated brands.

Conversely, in the case of radical innovations such as new chemical entities, home VCRs, DVD recorders, mobile phones and LCD screens, life-stages can last many years and the introduction stage can be very long, depending on the importance of the required environment reorganization for efficiently using the innovation.

In particular cases, the diffusion of a new product will depend on inertial or frictional factors, linked to the availability of information about its performance. In other cases, the duration of the introduction stage will be short and the growth stage will be anticipated if the new product is expected by the market, since it is suitable for satisfying widespread needs not yet resolved by the existing products. (Let us think about a new ethical drug which cures a serious and widespread disease.)

The duration of maturity and decline stages depends, instead, on the competitive pressure in the sector, particularly on the renewal rate of products.

The dynamics of sales along the cycle also depend on the decisions of developing and sustaining sales and physical distribution of the product. For example, the introduction phase can be reduced through an advertising campaign directed at emphasizing the attributes of a new product to customers, thereby overcoming the resistance to the innovation. A change in the sales network can also have a great influence and accelerate the rate of diffusion of the new product.

The decisions regarding prices are also very important. In the introduction and growth stages low prices can accelerate market development and delay the diffusion of competitors' products; in the decline stage, low prices can make the market less vulnerable to rival actions, reducing the speed of decline.

However, to choose a price policy carefully, the innovative firm has to consider not only the current characteristics of demand, along the various cycle stages, but also the effects of prices on the evolution of sales along the cycle. Thus, it is necessary to determine the pattern of prices, related to the various cycle phases, suitable for producing the maximum firm value.

Despite the actions for delaying the decline of sales, the life cycle of the product will end; inexorably new products will replace the oldest, these later being replaced by other more effective ones.

In this dynamic environment, a firm can regain a competitive advantage only if it succeeds in introducing new types of products or models, driving a new cycle of sales. But the investment in the new product will create value only if the pattern of prices and the pattern of quantities sold are appropriate for generating a present value of operating cash flows almost equal to the investment. Thus the duration of product life and the related pattern of prices are fundamental variables which make a good investment or not.

AN ANALYTICAL MODEL FOR EVALUATING PRODUCT INNOVATION STRATEGIES

To clarify the essential aspects of the problem, let us assume that product innovation consists of a new model or type of a basic product.

After a short introduction stage, we can consider that the new model will prevail in the market because it is new; the firm that introduces it will temporarily have a certain superiority over competitors. This permits the innovator to charge higher prices and also obtain bigger sales. But this superiority will be modified over time, because of the introduction of new types or models by rival firms, causing the progressive fall of sales and prices of the old product.

To express everything in analytical terms, consider that at the beginning a firm j obtains a volume of sales $Q(0)$ at a price $P(0)$ and has a unit cost $C(0)$, after the launch of the new product. At time 0, the *EBITDA* will be:

$$EBITDA(0) = Q(0) [P(0) - C(0)] \tag{5.1}$$

We assume that, after the launch of the new product, the sales $Q(t)$ will increase at a rate φ_1 for a period $T1$ (for example 2–3 years), at an annual rate φ_2 for a following period $T2$ and then that sales will decrease at a rate φ_3, because of the competitive pressure caused by the flows of new models introduced by rival firms.

The pattern of the firm sales, $Q(t)$, after the launch of the new model at time $t = 0$, can be represented by a function of time, as follows:

$$Q(t) = Q(0) (1 + \varphi_1)^t \qquad \text{for } 0 \ < t < \ T1$$

$$Q(t) = Q(T1) (1 + \varphi_2)^t \qquad \text{for } T1 \ < t \ < \ T2$$

$$Q(t) = Q(T2) (1 - \varphi_3)^t \qquad \text{for } T2 \ < t \tag{5.2}$$

We also suppose that the product price increases in time at a constant annual rate s, as the effect of inflation, and decreases at a rate γ, due to competition from the new products of rival firms:

$$P(t) = P(0) (1 + s - \gamma)^t \tag{5.3}$$

The unit operating cost of product $C(t)$ (before the deterioration cost) will increase at a rate s, due to inflation.

$$C(t) = C(0) (1 + s)^t \tag{5.4}$$

Because of these conditions, the function that expresses the *EBITDA* of the new product is:

$$EBITDA(t) = [P(0) (1 + s - \gamma)^t - C(0) (1 + s)^t] Q(t) \tag{5.5}$$

where: $m(t) = P(t) - C(t)$ is the unit margin.

Over time, the $EBITDA(t)$ declines, because of the fall in quantities sold and in prices (Figure 5.2). The duration of product life (T) is defined by the time in which the unit margin equals zero, passing to negative values, that is when the following condition is satisfied:

$$P(0) (1+s-\gamma)^T - C(0) (1+s)^T = 0 \tag{5.6}$$

From the equation (5.6), we can obtain the variable T.[1] Precisely it will be:

$$T = \frac{\log P(0) - \log C(0)}{\log(1+s) - \log(1+s-\gamma)} \tag{5.7}$$

The strategy of product innovation will create value when:

$$\sum_1^T [P(0) (1+s-\gamma)^t - C(0) (1+s)^t] \, Q(t) \, (1-\tau^*)/(1+\rho)^t$$
$$> I(0) + I_{MK}(0) + I_{R\&D}(0) \tag{5.8}$$

where: in addition to the already known symbols, τ^* is the adjusted tax rate on *EBITDA*, $I(0)$ the investment in production capacity, $I_{R\&D}$ the R&D investment and $I_{MK}(0)$ the marketing investment for the launch of the new product.

The expression indicates the value of the strategy as the net present value of the operating cash flows produced during the lifetime of the new product.

Note that the greater is γ, the shorter the duration T.

The firm value depends on the estimated environment trends (s, γ, φ), the investments required $I(0) + I_{MK}(0) + I_{R\&D}(0)$ and the cost of capital (ρ).

The model highlights that the value of a strategy depends primarily on the prices and the sales quantities of a new product, given the decreasing rate of sales φ, caused by the technical progress and the competitive pressure in the industry. In turn, prices and quantities depend on the intensity of product innovation with respect to rival products and thus on the success of R&D activities. The greater the unit margin, the longer the duration of the new product will be and, given the sales volumes, the greater the value of the strategy. Obviously, a different value of $Q(0)$ corresponds to each price $P(0)$, due to the demand elasticity of the new product. Price policy has, therefore, its constraints in market conditions.

The amount of investment required is also important for the innovation strategy creating value. In this respect, we note that the capital expenditure necessary for creating the new product varies from case to case, being strongly related to production technologies and to the intensity of technological progress. In some cases the required investment is very high, because the new product implies the change of the entire production line or plant, while in other cases it only involves the change of specific machines and equipment, such as moulds, shapes, part-holders, etc.

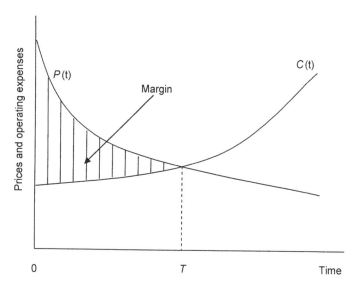

Figure 5.2   Dynamics of prices and costs of a new product launched at t = 0

Conversely, the investments in the marketing system are usually limited, since the renewal of the product only affects some components of the firm's structure. For example, it requires an increase in advertising expenses, in order to speed up the introduction and the growth of sales, but does not require changes in the sales network, or in the outbound logistic system or sales organization.

The proposed model allows the calculation of the value of the innovation strategy to be made. It is a matter of establishing an initial price $P(0)$, estimating the related amount of sales volumes $Q(0)$ and calculating the value of the strategy and the life of the new product. Different hypotheses on prices or quantities sold allow the calculation, through a simulation process, of the values of strategies which are consistent with different market situations.

The model emphasizes that the higher the declining rate of sales (φ) and the decline of unit margin (γ) are, the shorter the duration of the product life will be and the higher the starting price $P(0)$ of the new product.

The level of the starting margin on operative costs will also depend on the intensity of innovation of the new product, with respect to products of rivals.

The intensity of innovation will affect the shape of the demand curve and the price elasticity of the product as well.

In short, the investment in the new product is worthwhile if there are values of $P(0)$ and T that yield a net present value of the investment not less than zero, considering the dynamics of cash flows, caused by innovations and the competitive pressure of rival firms.

Note that not every innovation strategy has the same level of consistency with regard to the product life, prices and R&D investments, because the power in pricing is limited by the characteristics of product demand and the industry structure.

On one hand, price policy has to be subordinated to the product innovation strategy, since prices have to generate cash flows adequate for financing the investment necessary for achieving the objective. On the other hand, the innovation strategy has to be consistent with the price policies enabled by the structural conditions of the industry and demand.

Therefore, in highly dynamic environments, to continue creating value, a firm has to invest and prepare the introduction of a new product, while exploiting the success of the present product. In these conditions of competition, a mistake can cause an irreversible crisis in the firm. On this topic, D'Aveni (1994 p. 128) remembers that Gordon Moore, founder of Intel, said that his business 'lived on the edge of a precipice', because of continuous innovations and the pressure of competitors. After having projected a new microchip, Intel had to produce it rapidly and think about a new innovation, due to the pressure from competitors.

RADICAL PRODUCT INNOVATIONS: SALES DYNAMICS AND PRICE POLICIES

In the case of radical product innovation, for example a new chemical entity or a new product architecture or platform, the analytical conditions for the strategy creating value are similar to those we presented in the previous section. The value of the strategy will depend on the sales volumes during the life cycle of the product, the prices, the operating costs of the product and the total investment. On the relevance of the different variables, the ideas put forward in the previous section still hold true.

But, in the case considered here, the determination of the relevant variables is more difficult, with respect to the case of the innovation of the types or models of a basic product, because the sales along the life cycle of the new product are more difficult to plan. In particular, the pattern of sales is characterized by a longer life cycle, with introductory and growth stages going on some years.[2] The intensity of innovation can determine great opportunities in sales, but also big risks for the firm, because the resistance to changes can extend the time of diffusion of the new product (Grabowski and Vernon 1990).

In this context, the price policy assumes a very important role in creating value. The first innovator can fix very high prices and margins, gradually reducing them, so exploiting the superior performance of the new product with respect to competitors.[3] This policy will permit high cash flows to be obtained during the period the firm has a monopolistic position, but it will postpone the growth of the market and favour the introduction of new products from rivals. Conversely, the first innovator can fix low prices for the new product, favouring the rapid growth of the market and the reduction of production costs, by the increase of volumes, also reducing the competitive pressure of rivals.

In any case, the competitive advantage will be temporary; over time competitors will introduce similar or superior products, causing a progressive decline in the prices and margins of the first innovator. See, for example, the continuous declining of prices of many new electronic products, due to the more efficient production methods and the increasing pressure from competitors, as shown in Figures 5.3, 5.4 and 5.5.

In short, the alternative price policies of a new product are:

- the skimming prices policy
- the penetration prices policy.

The first consists in initially adopting very high prices and then gradually reducing them; the second is characterized by initially adopting low prices to quickly reach high volumes of sales. The advantage of one or the other depends on the price elasticity of demand for the new product.

A skimming prices policy is preferable when price elasticity is less than 1 and sales growth is delayed by social and economic factors reducing the diffusion of the new product. This policy allows the firm to enjoy the monopolistic position after the innovation, especially when innovation is protected, for example, by a patent (Melewicki and Sivakumar 2004).

Firms also adopt a skimming prices policy when elasticity of demand is unknown and there is only approximate information on the dynamics of production costs. In this situation this policy gives the firm a sort of protection, permitting it to exploit market segments which are not sensitive to prices and to obtain high cash flows, necessary for rapidly repaying R&D expenses.

However, a firm will gradually reduce prices because it can extract a rent from innovation only for a short time; this duration depends on the ability of competitors to imitate or innovate products.

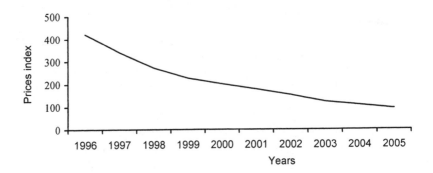

Source: US Department of Labor (2006).

Figure 5.3   Price dynamics of electronic computers: production prices index

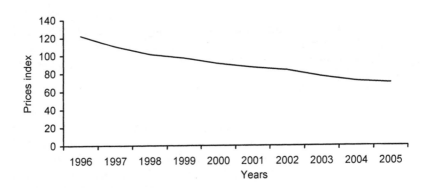

Source: US Department of Labor (2006).

*Figure 5.4   Price dynamics of semiconductors and related devices:
production prices index*

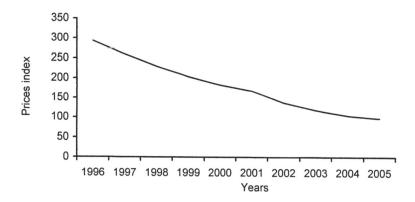

Source: US Department of Labor (2006).

*Figure 5.5   Price dynamics of computer storage devices: production prices
index*

Today, reverse engineering techniques permit the most technologically
advanced rivals to reproduce new products easily and quickly.[4] In addition, a
firm will reduce prices to prevent the entry of new firms and the introduction
of imitations.[5] Obviously, this reduction will be small and gradual if the new
product is effectively protected by patent.

The skimming prices policy has been adopted in various industries, in
particular the pharmaceutical industry (Reekie 1978; Steele 1964; Brooke
1975) and the electronics industry (see data shown in Table 5.1).

The alternative prices policy is represented by a penetration prices policy.
This policy is characterized by low prices in the introduction stage of the new
product. It is preferable, generally, when the new product presents a high
price elasticity, starting from the introduction and growth stages.

Sometimes, this policy is reinforced by scale economies in production and
distribution. This policy, directed at developing a mass market, also requires
consistent marketing and distribution investments.

A policy of price penetration was adopted by Ford in the 1920s, when the
car was in the introduction stage in the USA. The drastic price reduction
boosted the sales and this permitted production costs to be reduced and
margins to be increased. In recent times, penetration price policies have been

adopted by many firms, as we can see by industry data such as electronic consumer goods, personal computers, semiconductors, integrated analogical circuits and others. In the early personal computer industry, for example, Atari, TI and Commodore reduced prices at an annual rate of 29.9% between 1980 and 1983, in order to expand the market (Williamson 1992).

Table 5.1   Price dynamics of new electronic products

Industry	Period	Rate of variation of prices (mean % annual)
Consumer electronics	1982–89	–3.6
Microwave ovens	1982–89	–4.6
Integrated analogical circuits	1981–89	–4.8
Digital PBXs	1985–89	–4.9
Integrated circuits	1985–89	–4.9
Integrated electronic watches	1973–83	–10.0
Digital computers	1988–89	–10.3

Source: Williamson (1992).

Obviously the penetration policy must be carefully evaluated, because it can cause high costs and risks, minor profits or losses before it can work well, developing the sales quickly.

However, in the case of radical product innovations, to create value a firm also has to adopt a price policy over time which is consistent with sales quantities and operating costs, so as to obtain discounted cash flows not less than the total investment in the new product.

THE VALUE OF A PRODUCT INNOVATION STRATEGY: A SIMULATION

In this section we present a simulation of our model in order to better emphasize the influence of the most relevant variables on the strategy value.

We refer to the strategy of product innovation of a firm operating in the car industry. Data used are real and refer to a well known model of car launched in 1999 by a famous firm. The new product, available in two versions, salon and station wagon, relied on the elegance and the innovation of lines; it was designed for segment D, that is 22% of the European market.

The new model required a total investment of €400 million, 100 million of which were for the development and the engineering of the new product. The expected sales on the European market were equal to 60,000 cars per year, with a life cycle of six years. The sale started in September 1999; the basic price was set at €25,000. We also assume:

- an inflation rate equal to 2% per year;
- a launching price $P(0) = €17,500$;
- quantities sold in the first year $Q(0) = 60,000$; the quantities sold after the launch of the new product $Q(t)$ vary in the following way: increasing at a rate φ_1 equals 10% in the first two years, increasing at a rate φ_2 equals 5% in the following two years, decreasing at a rate φ_3 equals 10% in the 5th and 6th years and decreasing at a rate φ_4 equals 20% every year from the 7th to the 10th (Figure 5.6);
- a rate of price reduction for the aging of the product (γ) and a cost of capital ρ equal to 10%.

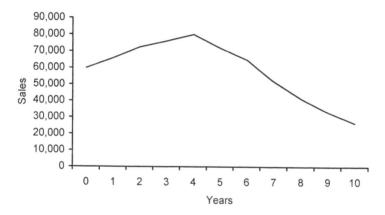

Figure 5.6   A simulation of the life cycle of a new product

Our model yields the results shown in Table 5.2. In case A the innovation strategy creates a new value of about €156m. Under the assumed conditions, the life of the new product (*T*) results as being equal to four years (Figure 5.7). All assumptions remaining constant, the value of the strategy becomes negative and equals €287m if the initial price can be increased to €20,000; the duration of life of the new product (*T*) rises to seven years (Case B). The value of the strategy becomes negative and equals €2m if the initial sales are equal to 60,000 units, but the competitive pressure requires reducing prices at 8% per year, for the aging of the product, to maintain the programmed sales (Case B). Table 5.2 shows the strategy values and the life duration of the new product with regard to the different hypotheses.

Table 5.2   The value of product innovation strategies: simulation data

	Case A	Case B	Case C
Rate of growth of cost and prices for inflation (s)	0.02	0.02	0.02
Rate of price reduction for the aging of the product (γ)	0.05	0.05	0.08
Rate of variation of product prices ($s-\gamma$)	−0.03	−0.03	−0.06
Cost of capital	0.10	0.10	0.10
Price of product $P(0)$ in €	17,500	20,000	20,000
Unit cost of production $C(0)$ in €	14,000	14,000	14,000
Quantities sold a $t=0$	60,000	60,000	60,000
Rate of variation of sales φ_1	+0.10	+0.10	+0.10
Rate of variation of sales φ_2	+0.05	+0.05	+0.05
Rate of variation of sales φ_3	−0.10	−0.10	−0.10
Rate of variation of sales φ_4	−0.20	−0.20	−0.20
Tax rate adjusted	0.25	0.25	0.25
Total investment (€/mill.)	400	400	400
Value of the strategy (€/mill.)	−156	+287	−2
Product life T (years)	4	7	4

The simulation proves that the value of the strategy is very sensitive to the decrease rate of the prices, because of the competitive pressure of new products, introduced by rivals. The success of the product innovation, expressed by the higher initial price, and the competitive pressure are, therefore, main factors affecting the value of the strategy.

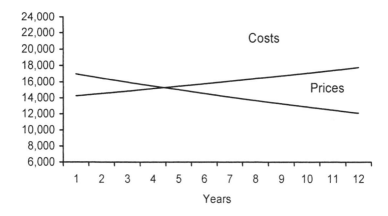

Figure 5.7   Dynamics of prices and costs of a new car (case A)

PRODUCT INNOVATION STRATEGIES AND THE RELIABILITY OF THE DEVELOPMENT PLAN

Usually, in a competitive environment the aging of models and types of product is programmed by the same firm that offers them to buyers. This behaviour permits the firm to reduce the risk of being overtaken by competitors or being late in product innovation. Therefore, instead of an estimated rate of decreasing sales, φ, as the expression of the competitive pressure due to product innovations by the rival firms, we can assume a programmed rate φ^*, an expression of the intensity of innovation by the considered firm. This rate is, therefore, a firm objective, not a market trend.

Under the assumed conditions, the firm can maintain the position of leader only if it is able to reach the innovation objectives at a level not inferior to that pursued by and obtained by rivals. A slowing down of R&D activities and a progressive reduction of the innovation flow will favour the offensive action of incumbent and potential rivals, causing the breakdown of the market share to the advantage of the most dynamic rivals.

However, the firm has no advantage in speeding up the renewal of the product, causing advanced aging, since this will prevent the firm from fully exploiting the opportunities of positive cash flows still coming from the existing product. Moreover, this strategy needs to increase R&D expenses with a higher risk of failure. Hence, it will be better to set the innovation objective maintaining a certain advantage with respect to the competitors and reducing the risk of unexpected innovations.

In every case the firm will have to sustain a level of R&D expenses at least sufficient for maintaining the rate of technical progress of the industry, and for introducing the new models of products required by the market. This minimum defensive level of R&D expenses differs from industry to industry; think for example of the high investments and the rapid life cycle of personal computers, software, electronic components for telecommunications, etc.

In these situations, price policy takes on a central role; it has to produce the cash flows necessary for sustaining the programmed objectives. Its consistency, with respect to the conditions of demand and industry, will confirm the reliability of the strategy. In fact, the possibility of sustaining the investments the plan requires depends on these variables.

As the model shown highlights, pursuing superior objectives in product innovations means intensifying the R&D expenses and reducing the life cycle of products. All this requires higher margins on the product and therefore higher prices and quantities sold (volume). But this has to be consistent with market conditions and especially with demand conditions and industry competition (incumbent and potential entrants).

All this implies that the structural changes of a firm must be evaluated on the basis of a consistent determination of prices policy and product innovation strategy, so that the plan can be reliable. In short, if the firm through its structural characteristics is not able to maintain price and renewal rate of products comparable with its rivals, it will have to quit the industry before bearing increasing losses and destruction of value. This has often happened in many sectors. The history of many firms provides evidence that under strong competitive pressure, in the absence of appropriate structural changes, income flows tend to decrease progressively over time and end up becoming negative.

For example, IBM early on obtained large benefits from the launch of new PCs and developed entry barriers and power over buyers and suppliers that extended these benefits for years. But these advantages in cost and quality or timing and know-how were eroded by the continuous actions of competitors and the reduction in price due to decreasing commodity costs; the cycles of new products became more and more compressed and maintaining a sustainable advantage was increasingly difficult. In the period 1995–2004 IBM exited or greatly re-emphasized its involvement in the consumer market, to concentrate on the enterprise market (server and mainframe market), where opportunities were superior. This company first left the sector of the desk PC and then that of the mobile PC, selling, on may 2005, the Personal

Computing Division to Lenovo, one of China's computer leaders. IBM made its choice: to be an innovation company in high-value markets, instead of being a high-volume player in desktop and laptop computers.

In the electronics industry recently (October 2007) Hitachi, a former pioneer of PC development, announced it was to abandon the game, because of the implacable competition depressing sales and margins. Some weeks before Sony had decided to leave the chip branch, selling it to its rival Toshiba, and Matsushita had handed over the control of JVC to Kenwood.

THE INTERNAL CONSTRAINTS TO PRODUCT INNOVATION STRATEGY

The possibility of carrying out product innovations depends, above all, on the technological and organizational know-how of the firm. This stems from individual skills and learning-by-doing processes.

In effect, new technologies are built on existing skills and on the internal activities of the firm, according to a cumulative process. Creating a new product principally requires human resources with particular skills in the organization and the solution of production problems.[6]

But, in the case of radical innovations, a firm also has to develop new resources and competences to be successful. This is not simple, because highly developed competences in some technologies often determine the core rigidities to the acquisition and development of the new competences required for innovative products and processes (Leonard-Barton 1992). Many firms experienced these difficulties, such as Digital Equipment in minicomputers, Xerox in copiers and Olivetti in typewriters. Sometimes, when radical changes occur in a sector or when entirely new business opportunities arise, new firms are better positioned than established ones (Grant 1998). These companies not only have to acquire new competences, but they have to dismiss existing ones and dismantle old structures. Among new successful companies during the 1990s in the PC sector, we can note Dell, Acer and Compaq.

Capability at the top management level is particularly important in process innovation. Innovation strategy requires capability in organization and personnel leadership and a clear vision of the future. In particular, the entrepreneur must define the objectives to reach, with far-sightedness and consistency, correctly interpreting the changes of the industry and the environment. He must be capable of organizing and controlling the activities of managers in charge of the R&D activities and efficiently realize the required investments.[7]

The dimension of the firm is the other important factor influencing innovation. The positive impact on innovation is due to the more favourable conditions in which R&D activities can be carried out: scale economies of R&D, risk reduction through project diversification, advantages in product distribution. In many industries the distribution of products is the most difficult barrier to overcome for the smaller firms.

Financial resources are also important for creating innovations. The high risk of R&D investment requires that these be financed essentially through equity and particularly through cash flows produced by current operations. The innovation strategy will depend, therefore, on the level of the operating incomes and the efficiency of the structure of the existing firm, as well as on the conditions characterizing the structure of the industry.

STRATEGY FOCUS: PRODUCT INNOVATION STRATEGIES IN SOME RELEVANT INDUSTRIES

Product Innovation Strategies in the Car Industry

The car industry is a classical example of an industry characterized by a continuous flow of product innovations. They are principally innovations regarding models and types of a basic product, driven by technical progress and change in customer behaviour patterns.

In recent times, the life of a product has been reduced by increasing competition among companies. This has made firms increasingly involved in R&D activities developing new products, absolutely necessary for restoring the competitive advantage and the market share.

The product innovation strategy of the Fiat Group

The importance of product innovation is pointed out by the CEO of Fiat (2004 and 2006 Fiat annual reports). He declared:

> In 2004, Fiat Auto continued to pursue a strategy focused on upgrading its model line-up and increasing its competitiveness in anticipation of 2005, when the Sector was to launch several brand-new models in market segments that are important for the profitability of its brands. The most important new launches will be those of the New Fiat Punto, the New Fiat Croma, the Alfa Romeo 159 and the Alfa Romeo Brera. During the last quarter of 2004, the Lancia Musa was presented to customers in Italy, with its commercial launch in the other European markets scheduled for early 2005. The Lancia Musa, a sophisticated and elegant car, marks another step forward in Fiat Auto's commitment to the environment. The available fuel-efficient, low emission engines comply with the Euro 4 emissions limits. The Fiat Panda family of cars was expanded with the introduction of a Multijet version, which is powered by this innovative diesel

engine, and towards the end of the year by a gasoline-fuelled 4×4 model. A
Multijet version of the 4×4 model will follow in 2005. The Sector also expanded
the model lines of the Fiat Idea (a version with a Dualogic transmission was
added), the Fiat Punto (the Connect version with a standard satellite navigation
system has become available) and the Fiat Stilo (a version with a 100 hp JTD
engine is now being offered). Between June and October, in addition to the
Lancia Musa mentioned above, Fiat Auto launched the New Fiat Multipla, the
Alfa Cross-wagon Q4 (an entry in the all-wheel-drive market niche) and the
restyled Alfa 147. In the light commercial vehicle segment, the Sector introduced
the New Scudo, which will play a key role in enhancing brand profitability, and
rounded out the Ducato line. In 2004, Fiat Auto and Opel AG signed a contract
whereby Fiat will use General Motors Epsilon architecture for the production of
the New Fiat Croma, which was unveiled in a world preview at the Geneva
International Motor Show in March 2005. Another contract, signed with Suzuki,
will help Fiat enter the SUV segment with a jointly developed, Fiat-branded
vehicle that will be manufactured by Suzuki in Hungary' (Fiat, Annual Report,
2006 p. 64).

In 2004 Fiat Auto reported €19,695 million net revenues with 1,766,000
vehicles sold over the world. Total operating loss rose €818 million and the
main product, the Fiat Punto, was in the decline stage after a life cycle of 11
years (Figure 5.8).

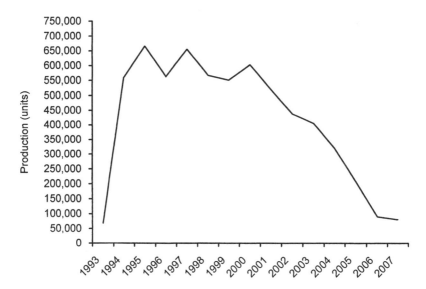

Source: Our elaboration on ANFIA data.

*Figure 5.8   Dynamics of production and sales of the Fiat Punto model
(number of cars)*

The new models launched in 2005 and 2006 made a spectacularly successful turnaround possible, with increasing volumes, revenues and profits. In particular, the positive sales performances during 2006 stemmed from the growing success of new models that had been introduced previously, first and foremost the Grande Punto and Panda (Table 5.3) as well as other models that were introduced during the year to enrich the product line of the three brands (Fiat, Lancia, Alfa Romeo).

Thanks to the success of new models, Fiat Auto reported in 2006 net revenues of €23,702 million (up 21.3% from 2005) with 1,980,300 automobiles and light commercial vehicles delivered, with a growth of 16.7% from 2005.

Table 5.3   Sales of new Fiat models after the launch (number of cars)

	2005	2006	2007E
Panda	220,000	237,000	250,000
G. Punto	74,000	344,000	360,000

Source: Fiat, Annual Report, 2006.

Trading performance in this year was positively impacted by the growing success of new models and in particular the Fiat Grande Punto and the Panda, the Alfa Romeo 159 (sedan and sport-wagon), the Brera and the new Lancia Ypsilon, as well as the light commercial vehicles, such as the *New Ducato* and the New Doblò.

In total in the years 2005–2006 Fiat launched 22 new vehicles, as new and updated models. In the next three years, 2007–2010, Fiat has planned to enrich the range of products by 23 new models and as many updated ones.

Risk and return in product innovation strategy at the Renault Group
The risk in innovating a product can be very high, especially if the old product represents a high share of the firm market.

The replacement of the medium car Renault 19 is an emblematic example. This model, in its variants, had sold more than 3 million units; for six years it had been the most sold car in the C segment in France and for five years the most imported car in Germany. After a life of six years this model was replaced by the new model Mégane. This new car opened a new important chapter in the history of the French house. It found a market (segment C) that had increased its share in Europe from 27% in 1985 to 32% in 1994, becoming since 1992 the most important segment in Europe.

For the new Mégane, the expected sales were prudent: 4 million cars in seven years, corresponding to a market share of 11% of the C segment in Europe, the same share Renault had on the total market. To reach this target Renault had invested approximately €2.3 billion (13.8 billion francs in 1995).

The Mégane was offered in five different bodywork solutions, five door saloon, sport, followed in 1996 by the four-door model, and by the mono-volume (the only one available on the market). In 18 months the launch of the open top was programmed. The new motors were represented by a petrol motor 1.6 lt with 90 CV and a 2.0 lt 150 CV, in addition to the recently known 1.4 lt 75 CV and 2.0 lt with 115 CV. They had programmed, moreover, a new diesel 1.9 lt with 96 CV and a new turbo-diesel. The innovations for safety were numerous: a system of controlled stop, anti-intrusion devices, etc.

Product Innovation Strategy in the Cosmetic Industry: the L'Oréal Case

The cosmetics industry is another example of an industry characterized by a continuous flow of product innovations.

In the beauty business, new products are a necessity being required by customers. Most of all, new products are incremental innovations in types or models of a basic product. Most experts agree that real breakthroughs are a rare event. In most cases science serves the humble task of improving the texture of a product. In other cases a new product uses a new raw material, so the new product is not only more effective but also biodegradable, non-bio-cumulative and non-eco-toxic.

L'Oréal is a leading firm in this industry. Founded in 1907 by chemist Eugene Schneller, inventor of the first synthetic hair dye, L'Oréal reveals its research roots. Two of L'Oréal's four CEOs have been scientists and the company's research in skin care, hair products and cosmetics yields an average 300 patent applications a year.

In 2006 the Group obtained €15,790 million consolidated sales, (+8.7%) and €2,541 million operating profits (+12.1%) with a share of the world cosmetics market equal to 15.6%. As the CEO declares, 'the first cylinder of the group's growth engine is technological innovation'.

L'Oréal is an international company with a large portfolio of products in three fundamental areas: cosmetics with €15,011 million sales in 2006, The Body Shop with €435 million sales and dermatology with €344 million sales.

In each area of cosmetics this company has diversified and complementary brands (L'Oréal, Kerastase, Redken, Matrix, Garnier, Maybelline, Vichy, Lancome, Biotherm, Helena Rubistein, Giorgio Armani, Cacharel (perfume) Ralph Lauren (perfume), Kiehl's, etc.), to penetrate and conquer new markets. The consolidated sales by the business segment, in 2006, are shown in Table 5.4.

Table 5.4   L'Oréal, cosmetics business segments: 2006 consolidated sales (€m)

Total cosmetics sales	15,011
Skincare	3,850
Haircare	3,633
Make-up	3,123
Hair colorants	2,342
Perfumes	1,572
Other	402

Source: Annual Report, 2006.

The product innovation strategy is the core of its competitive strategy. It can be summarized in this objective: *updating roughly 50% of the product line every three years*.

L'Oréal also obtained radical innovations in cosmetics. In the 1980s and 1990s it created richer-looking, less harsh hair colouring products that enabled L'Oréal to reach number 1 in the global market and rival once-dominant Clairol in the US. In 1997 a newly designed curled brush enabled L'Oréal's Maybelline Inc. to be the first major seller in mascara in China.

Recently, L'Oréal's laboratories developed Pro-Xylane™, a new anti-ageing compound, made using green chemistry techniques; according to the management it will become a milestone in the history of anti-aging skincare. Introduced into the group's core brands, it should give them a major technological advantage in conquering the 'seniors' market, a strategic opportunity in all developed countries.

And the quest for breakthroughs continues. L'Oréal scientists are searching for a way to prevent hair from greying and ultimately make hair grow where there is none. The management believes there will be new products in ten years.

Over the past ten years L'Oréal has pumped $3.2 billion into research and development. For maintaining the flow of new products, at the end of 1999 2,147 researchers worked in the general headquarters in Paris, more than all workers in the French factories. At the end of 2006 total research employees were 2,961; the research investments in 2006 were equal to €533 million, with 569 patents registered in the same year.

Rivals in the cosmetics industry, such as Procter & Gamble, Beiersdorf, and Revlon, keep their labs busy, too. They all know the game's rules!

Product Innovation Strategies in the Pharmaceutical Industry: the Novartis Case

Product innovation is the winning weapon for successfully competing in the pharmaceutical industry. The importance of R&D in the pharmaceutical industry is confirmed by the R&D expenses data of the four major international firms in 2002 (Table 5.5).

The ability of firms operating in this industry to increase their business and to replace any lost sales, due to the loss of exclusivity for their products in the future, depends upon the ability of the R&D activities to identify and develop high-potential breakthrough products and to bring them onto the market.

Given that the development and regulatory approval for a new pharmaceutical product frequently takes more than ten years and can involve costs of over US$1 billion, the need for efficient and productive R&D activities is critical to the continued business success of firms.

The quality of the current development pipeline in a firm reflects investments made in R&D activities, in many cases more than ten years ago, as well as recent acquisitions and licensing collaborations.

Table 5.5   R&D expenses of major pharmaceutical companies (2002)

Company	R&D expenses in million $
Pfizer	4,847
Glaxo-SKL	3,702
Johnson & Johnson	3,600
Merck	2,456

Source: Companies' annual reports.

Novartis represents a clear example of a firm competing by product innovation and strongly involved in R&D. Novartis defines its mission in this way: 'we want to discover, develop and successfully market innovative products to cure diseases, ease suffering and enhance the quality of life'. This company is a world leader in providing medicines to protect health, prevent and treat diseases and to improve well-being. It offers a wide range of healthcare products through its Pharmaceuticals, Vaccines and Diagnostics, Sandoz and Consumer Health divisions.

In 2006 the Novartis Group recorded $37,020 million total net sales, $7,202 million net income and $4,045 million free cash flow. The R&D expenses reached $5,364 million, that is 14.5% of net sales.

Group sales by division are as follows: 61% pharmaceutical products, 3% vaccines and diagnostics, 16% Sandoz and 20% consumer health products. The net sales of the pharmaceutical division are represented in Table 5.6.

Table 5.6   Novartis pharmaceuticals division net sales, by therapeutic area (2006, US$ million)

Total division net sales		22,576
Cardiovascular		7,120
▪ Strategic franchise products	6,472	
▪ Mature products	648	
Oncology		5,909
Neuroscience		3,097
▪ Strategic franchise products	2,657	
▪ Mature products	440	
Respiratory & Dermatology		3,097
▪ Strategic franchise products	1,837	
▪ Mature products	123	
Arthritis/Bone/Gastrointestinal/Urinary		2,251
▪ Strategic franchise products	725	
▪ Mature products	1,526	
Infectious diseases, Transplantation & Immunology		1,514
▪ Strategic franchise products	1,248	
▪ Mature products	266	
Ophthalmic		726

Source: Novartis, Annual Report 2006.

Note that the largest part of $22,576 million total net sales in 2006 are represented by the strategic franchise products ($19,573 million), while the mature products add up to $3,003 million. That clearly indicates the importance of innovative products.

The business vision is declared by the Novartis Chairman and CEO in the 2006 annual report:

In these industry conditions, business as usual is no longer a viable long-term option. Identifying and addressing the needs of patients remains at the forefront of all that we do. This includes taking a serious look at the economic and political realities in which patients live because this plays a major role in determining how products are made available to them. This is why our business portfolio systematically reflects the dynamically changing healthcare market: growing demand for innovative medicine (Pharmaceuticals), the rising support for greater use of cheaper generics (Sandoz), the increasingly prominent role of vaccines (Vaccine and Diagnostics) and greater empowerment of patients (Consumer Health).

In 2006, the company defined 'investing vigorously in R&D to continue bringing new and innovative products to the market' (2006 Annual Report, p. 7) as a priority. The strategy of product innovation remains, therefore, the core of the Novartis business model. Important results have been produced from this strategy. We quote the extraordinary success of the antihypertensive medicine Diovan ($4.2 billion sales in 2006), expected to become the top-selling medication for high blood pressure worldwide (Table 5.7).

But the radical innovation is the product Gleevec (Glivec outside the USA); that is the Novartis breakthrough for chronic myeloid leukaemia. Gleevec is one of the most effective new cancer therapies going; launched in May 2001 in the USA and then in the rest of the world, it recorded sales of over $3 billion in 2007, after only five years of life (Figure 5.9).

Table 5.7   Novartis pharmaceuticals division top 10 products, net sales, 2006

Brands	Therapeutic area	$m	% change
Diovan/Co-Diovan	Hypertension	4,223	+15
Gleevec/Glivec	Chronic myeloid leukaemia	2,554	+18
Lotrel	Hypertension	1,352	+26
Zometa	Cancer complications	1,283	+5
Lamisil (group)	Fungal infections	978	−14
Neoral/Sandimmun	Transplantation	918	−4
Sandostatin	Acromegaly	915	+2
Lescol	Cholesterol reduction	725	−5
Trileptal	Epilepsy	721	+17
Femara	Breast cancer	719	+34
Top ten products	Total	14,388	+10

Source: Novartis, Annual Report 2006.

From 2000 to 2007 Novartis filed 17 new ethical drugs in the USA, more than any other big pharmaceutical company in the world. This innovation strategy produced a continuous increase in net sales, operating incomes and cash flows from 2003 to 2007.

On 26 February 2008, the market capitalization reached $124 billion, reflecting the high growth rate of sales and cash flows. To implement this strategy more than 4,300 scientists and technology experts work in the research organization of Novartis. Key areas of development are oncology and cardiovascular diseases.

At the end of 2006 about 140 development projects filled the Novartis Pharma pipeline, with a significant number of launches planned for 2007 and 2008. Among these are 50 new molecular entities (NMEs) and 88 life-cycle management projects with new indications or formulations.

In 2006, over 20 new projects were added to the pipeline, in cardiovascular, cancer and neurological areas of R&S. In this period other new products received approval from the US Food and Drug Administration and many innovative compounds reached the late stage of development.

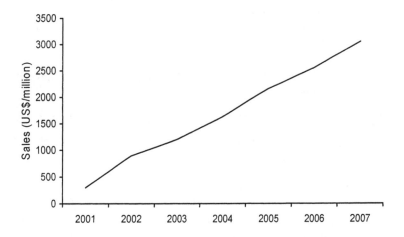

Source: Novartis Annual Reports.

Figure 5.9   Sales of the new product Gleevec (Novartis)

The Group has consistently had one of the highest R&D investment rates in the industry as a percentage of net sales, reflecting its commitment to bring innovative and differentiated products to the market. In 2006, Novartis invested a total of $5.4 billion in research and development, an 11% increase over 2005. Funding requirements for R&D activities are likely to continue to grow in the future. These investments, however, are critical for the continuing success of Novartis. As a result of past investments, Novartis was able to successfully launch a number of new products in 2006, in particular Exjade, Prexige and Xolair.

Subject to obtaining necessary regulatory approvals, Novartis is planning for multiple new product launches in the Pharmaceuticals Division in 2007–2008 and it expects some of these products to generate peak annual sales of over $1 billion. These products include Tekturna/Rasilez and Exforge for hypertension, Galvus for type 2 diabetes, Tasigna for cancer and Lucentis for blindness.

Product Innovation Strategies in the Consumer Electronics Industry: Sony and Apple

In 2003 Sony was the world's largest consumer electronics company, but its sales and profits had been falling since the end of the 1990s. In 2003 Sony shares fell by 25% after large quarterly losses. Sony announced it would cut jobs and lower the cost of its products.

Despite these actions, by 2005 the company was still in trouble: profits in the electronics and games division were falling and the company had lost out in areas in which it should have had a strong lead.

Sony had grown by inventing blockbuster products that have transformed the way we live and play: the tape recorder in 1950, the transistor radio in 1955, the Trinitron color TV in 1969, the Walkman in 1979, the CD player in 1982, the camcorder in 1983, the digital camera in 1988 and the PlayStation video game console in 1994. Each of these products not only achieved a great success, but created entirely new markets.

The company that had pioneered portable music players with the Walkman was left in the dust by the new Apple iPod in 2005.

Sony's choice of using only proprietary technology meant that Sony machines were not able to play MP3 files, as required by most people who download music. As the new CEO said, in order to revitalize the company, it was necessary not just to reduce costs, but to promote creativity, with new ideas and new products (Berger 2005).

To confirm the importance of product innovation consider the impressive value creation through Apple's product innovation strategy with the new iPod. This new product is the most important success in the recent history of Apple. It is a new digital music portable reader, with a high memory capacity, Windows compatible. Music downloaded through Apple iTunes can be transferred onto iPod without files being converted into another digital format.[7] This gives iPod a strong competitive advantage over competitors.

Launched on 23 February 2001, iPod remained compatible only with Apple Mac computers until 2003. After the opening to the PC world, iPod rapidly became a mass product.

Apple sold 51.6 million units of the iPod product family in 2007 and 10.6 million in the first three months of 2008, obtaining a share in the MP3 world market approximately equal to 80% (Table 5.8 and Figure 5.10).[8] Price policies also helped the rapid diffusion on the market (Figure 5.11).

In 2008 the enterprise value of Apple was estimated by independent research providers at about $152 billion and analysts calculate the value of the iPod division as being approximately half of this.

However, the maturity stage seems to have already arrived and new products will soon be necessary for creating value.

Table 5.8   *Apple net sales and the contribution of the iPod product family*

Fiscal years ending September	2001	2002	2003	2004	2005	2006	2007
Total net sales (million $)	5,363	5,742	6,207	8,279	13,931	19,315	24,006
Total net income (million $)		65	57	266	1,328	1,989	3,496
Years after the iPod launch		1	2	3	4	5	6
Net sales by iPod products (million $)	0	143	345	1,306	4,540	7,676	8,305
iPod unit sales (000)	0	381	939	4,416	22,497	39,409	51,630
Net sales per iPod unit sold ($)	0	375	367	296	202	195	161

Source: Apple Annual Reports, 2001–2007.

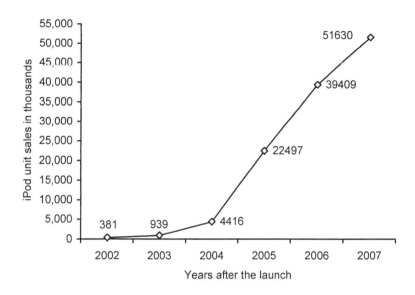

Source: Apple Annual Reports 2001–2007.

Figure 5.10   *Unit sales of the iPod product family after its launch in 2001*

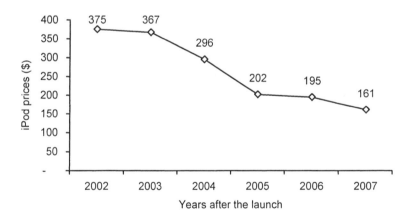

Source: Apple Annual Reports, 2001–2007.

Figure 5.11   *Price dynamics of the iPod product family after the launch in 2001*

Product Innovation Strategy: the Case of Geox

The Geox Group goes down in history as one of Italian industry's greatest success stories. Geox started up in 1995 as a small footwear company owned by the family Mario Moretti Polegato. Thanks to the inventiveness and determination of its founder, it created a technological innovation: a micro-porous membrane, placed on top of a sole, that makes the shoe able to breathe, but maintaining its water proofness (Geox leather and rubber patents).

After the introduction of this innovation, at the end of the 1990s, the company rapidly grew over the national borders, combining the revolutionary breathable and waterproof technology with Italian style, offering a collection of fashionable and functional footwear for women, men and children. In 2004 Geox was listed on the Milan Stock Exchange with remarkable success (Table 5.9).

Table 5.9   Geox key financials

Key operating data (€ million)	2006	2005	2004	2003	2002	2001
Net sales	612.3	455.0	340.1	254.1	180.3	147.6
Growth rate %	*35*	*34*	*34*	*41*	*22*	
EBITDA	153.5	121.0	87.1	50.0	31.1	16.1
EBITDA %	*25.1*	*26.6*	*25.6*	*19.7*	*17.3*	*10.9*
EBIT	134.9	102.9	72.8	38.7	23.9	11.9
EBIT %	*22.0*	*22.6*	*21.4*	*15.2*	*13.3*	*8.1*
PBT	133.9	106.1	68.5	33.8	19.5	9.9
PBT %	*21.9*	*23.3*	*20.1*	*13.3*	*10.8*	*6.7*
Net income	97.3	75.3	52.8	30.7	19.4	7.5
Net income %	*15.9*	*16.5*	*15.5*	*12.1*	*10.8*	*5.1*
Shareholders' equity	276.6	203.8	145.9	68.8	38.5	18.7
Market value	3,000	2,400	1,500			

Source: Geox Annual Reports.

In recent years, Geox has grown rapidly around the world and today it does business in 68 countries, with $612 million sales and more than 20 million pairs of shoes sold. Its foreign sales, amounting to 58% of its total, are mainly realized in Germany, France, Spain and the USA. Today, Geox distributes its products through over 10,000 multi-brand sales points and a network of over 700 single brand Geox shops, the latter being the flagships of the Geox brand in the world's main cities.

The innovation strategy rapidly created an impressive value for shareholders; the high *EBITDA* and the high expected rate of growth determined a market capitalization of €3 billion at the end of 2006, against a book value of equity equal to €277 million.

Geox continues to invest in R&D, in order to maintain its competitive advantage; at the end of 2006 40 patents were waiting in the pipeline to be launched on the market.

NOTES

1. The condition $P(0) (1 + s - \gamma)^T = C(0) (1+s)^T$ is equal to:

$$\left(\frac{1+s}{1+s-\gamma} \right)^T = \frac{P(0)}{C(0)}$$

Expressing this equation in logarithms with base $\alpha = (1 + s)/(1 + s - \gamma)$, we obtain an equivalent equation that permits obtaining the variable T as:

$$T = \log_\alpha (P(0)/C(0)) = \log_\alpha e \log (P(0)/C(0)) = \frac{\log (P(0)/C(0))}{\log \alpha}$$

$$T = \frac{\log P(0) - \log C(0)}{\log(1 + s) - \log(1 + s - \gamma)}$$

2. Bass (1969 and 1980) uses an epidemic model for explaining the diffusion of many durable consumer products in the American market. It is a growth model that can be applied only to the first acquisitions of a new product, not considering the renewal demand. A more complex model has been developed by Robinson and Lakhani (1975). These authors also consider the dynamic of product cost according to a typical 'learning curve'. On this basis the authors determine the optimal price path that maximizes the actual value of profits.

3. For analysing the determinants of radical product innovations see: Chandy and Tellis (1998); Martins and Terblanche (2003); Herrmann, Tomczak and Befurt (2006).

4. Thurow (1992, p. 44), considering the development of 'reverse engineering' and the consequent ease in reproducing new products, points out that the most durable bases of the competitive advantage are represented in the present time by the new process technologies, more than the new product technologies. After having mentioned cases of products such as videocameras and video and CD recorders, he underlines that the inventor of a new product does not obtain a great result if he is not able to produce it at the minimum cost.

5. The prices reduction in the introduction and growth stage will be larger if a high rate of technical progress in production methods and techniques will join with the considered conditions.
6. On the characteristics of innovative processes, see: Amendola and Gaffard (1988).
7. The importance of managerial excellence is underlined by Zirger and Maidique (1990) in an interesting study on innovation of high-tech products. The authors, who examined 330 new products in the electronics industry in order to understand the factors of success, found that excellence in management was the principal factor.
7. With iTunes Apple revolutionized the music industry through an agreement with the five major disco music companies. This agreement allows Apple to sell music through an Internet shop. The music is downloaded from the website and can be played by an iPod or a computer or copied onto a CD.
8. The iPod product family is made up of iPod Photo, iPodU2, iPodshuffle and iPodnano.

6. Creating value through integrated innovation strategies

INTRODUCTION AND OBJECTIVES

In Chapters 4 and 5 we presented two alternative strategy models, the first based on productivity increment objectives, the second based on renewal product objectives. Generally, the model based on the innovation of process prevails in scale-intensive sectors, whereas the model based on product innovation is typical of high technology sectors and those ones depending on fashion.

However, there are a lot of sectors where both product and process innovations are important. To extend the analysis, in this chapter we consider the firm pursuing both objectives of product innovation and productivity, with an integrated (mixed) strategy.[1] The analysis emphasizes the significant variables and the circumstances in which a mixed strategy can create sustainable value.

It points out that it is necessary for the firm to maintain a precise strategic identity to be successful, exploiting to the utmost its resources and competencies.

ENVIRONMENT TRENDS AND INNOVATIONS OF PRODUCT AND PROCESS

There are industries where the environment trends are characterized either by product or process innovations. The two types of innovations are so important that it is necessary for the firm to simultaneously adopt an integrated strategy, capable of producing both new products and productivity increments.

Only by investing at the same time in the two types of innovations will a firm will be able to hold technological leadership and the capability of creating value over a long period.

Consider, for example, high-tech sectors such as computers, microprocessors, video and radio fittings, wireless telephony and consumer electronics, where in the last 15 years there have been average growth rates of productivity in two digits, matched with high renewal rates of product innovation. In these sectors, innovations of product and process are combined in an organic way, as a consequence of microelectronic development.

But also in some maturing industries, such as automobiles, consumer electronics and appliances, high renewal rates of products and types are joined up with significant rates of productivity growth (an average of 3–5% a year).

In the automotive sector, we cite the case of Toyota, pursuing at the same time both a cost-leadership strategy, based on continual innovations of methods and productive processes, and a product innovation strategy, with new models of cars, in order to answer the varying consumer demands and the dynamics of technological progress (Baba 1989; Dess et al. 1995).

In the consumer electronics industry, a fair example is given by Sony, pursuing a strategy of both product innovation and costs reduction by the introduction of new productive technologies (Baba 1989).

THE EVALUATION OF AN INTEGRATED PRODUCT AND PROCESS INNOVATIONS STRATEGY

The value of an integrated strategy principally depends on the dynamics of expected cash flows produced by the new product and the new technical structure.

To represent analytically the conditions for a mixed strategy creating value, we assume the following functions of relevant variables:

(a) product cost $C_j(t)$ rising over time, because of the inflation rate (s):

$$C_j(t) = C_j(0) (1 + s)^t \qquad (6.1)$$

(b) product prices $P(t)$ rising over time because of the inflation rate (s) and decreasing, because of the aging of the product with respect to competitors' new products (γ) and the reducing costs of new products as a consequence of new production processes, with lower costs (δ):

$$P(t) = P(0) (1 + s - \gamma - \delta)^t \qquad (6.2)$$

(c) sales of the new product $Q(t)$ rising after its introduction and then diminishing at a rate φ because of its progressive aging with regard to the new products launched on the market by competitors:

$$Q_j(t) = Q_j(0) (1 - \varphi)^t \qquad (6.3)$$

It is important to note that the progressive reduction of *EBITDA* is determined by the increasing superiority of the new products of rivals, and the reduction of prices due to the reduction in cost caused by the introduction of new production technologies (Figure 6.1).

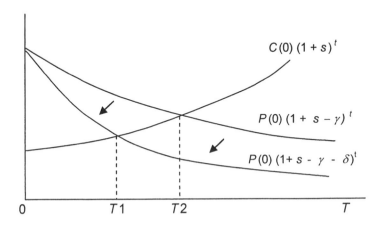

Figure 6.1   Product costs, prices and margins in highly dynamic industries

The conditions for an integrated strategy creating value are expressed by the following relations:

$$\sum_{t=1}^{T} \{[P(0) (1+ s - \gamma - \delta)^t - C_j(0) (1+ s)^t] Q(0) (1- \varphi)^t (1- \tau^*) / (1+ \rho)^t \}$$

$$- [I(0) + I_{MK}(0) + I_{R\&D}(0)] \geq 0 \qquad (6.4)$$

$$P(0) (1+ s - \gamma - \delta)^T - C_j(0) (1 + s)^T = 0 \qquad (6.5)$$

where, in addition to the well-known symbols, $I(0)$ is the investment in the new plant, $I_{R\&D}(0)$ is the investment in R&D and $I_{MK}(0)$ the investment in marketing.

From the equation (6.5) we can obtain T. [2] Precisely:

$$T = \frac{\log P(0) - \log C(0)}{\log(1 + s) - \log(1 + s - \gamma - \delta)} \qquad (6.6)$$

Note that the greater are γ and δ, the shorter T. Therefore, the advantage of the innovation strategy depends on the required investment, the tendencies of the industry, expressed by the rates φ, γ, δ, and s, and on the prices policy, according to the relations pointed out.

This model shows that, sales being equal, the higher the price of the new product, the higher the per unit margin will be and the longer the life of the new product and the greater the value of the strategy.

Obviously, each price level $P(0)$ of the new product produces a different quantity sold, $Q(0)$, in relation to the elasticity of the new product demand and consequently to the success of the product innovation. Therefore the limits of the prices policy are determined by market conditions and the success of the innovative processes.

Product life (and thus the plant's life) depends not only on the product innovation rate, which influences γ, but also on the renewal rate of productive processes which affects δ. Thus, the deterioration process of revenues is stressed by the cumulative effect due to product and process innovations.

This explains the strong reduction in the life of a product which has occurred in many sectors over the last few years, such as computers, microprocessors and radio and video fittings, where product innovation is continual and matched by a significant process innovation.

The size of the required investment for implementing the strategy is also important. Incidentally, we observe that the investments in the technical structure (the fixed capital) for the realization of the new product can be very different, strictly depending on the technologies adopted and the technical progress. In some cases the innovation of the product requires only the change of specific machines and equipment, such as moulds, shapes, equipment, etc.; in other cases, it implies the change of the whole line of production, or even the adoption of a new technology and the construction of a new plant.

The investments for the new product also include the goodwill required to make the new product known and quickly reach the sales target. Note that the sales target $Q(0)$ also depends on the price of the new product; the higher it will be, the lower the sales (quantities) and vice versa.

As the analytic model shows, it is not easy to compete successfully in the long run, especially when the rate of technical advance related to products and processes is high. That means, in fact, conditions of quick deterioration of the competitive advantage and short periods in which the innovative firms may benefit from the advantage.

In order to estimate the value of the strategy in an analytical way, it is useful to proceed by trial and error. It is a matter of calculating an initial price $P(0)$, estimating the matching value of $Q^*(0)$ on the basis of market research, and calculating the strategy value, considering that a product's life depends on these quantities. By repeating these attempts it is possible to find, through a simulation process, the values of $P(0)$ and T, consistent with the market conditions satisfying the relations as above.

If the strategy value is negative, because of the environment trends and the market conditions, it will be necessary to revise the investment plan and consider a new development strategy. If the expected income flow does not produce adequate yield on the invested capital, the best solution will be leaving the industry and liquidating the firm.

THE VALUE OF AN INTEGRATED INNOVATION STRATEGY: A SIMULATION

In this section we present a simulation of our model in order to better emphasize the influence of the most relevant variables on the strategy value.

We refer to the strategy of integrated innovation of a firm operating in the electronics industry. The data refer to a new product model, with a total investment of €300 million for the development and the engineering (Table 6.1). We also assume:

- an inflation rate s equal to 2% per year;
- a launching product price $P(0) = $ €800.00, or €1000.00;
- quantities sold in the first year $Q(0) = 500,000$; increasing at a rate φ_1 = 8% in the first two years; increasing at a rate φ_2 = 4% in the following two years, decreasing at a rate φ_3 = 10% in the 5th and 6th years and decreasing at a rate φ_4 = 20% every year from the 7th to the 12th;
- a rate of price reduction for the aging of the product γ equal to 10% or 5% ;
- a rate of price reduction for the process innovations (δ) equal to 3%;
- a cost of capital ρ equal to 10%.

Our model yields the results shown in Table 6.1.

In case A the innovation strategy creates a negative value of about €57 million and the life of the new product (T) results as being equal to five years (Figure 6.2).

Table 6.1   The value of integrated innovation strategies: simulation data

	Case A	Case B	Case C
Rate of growth of cost and prices for inflation (s)	0.02	0.02	0.02
Rate of price reduction for the aging of the product (γ)	0.1	0.05	0.1
Rate of price reduction for process innovation (δ)	0.03	0.03	0.03
Rate of variation of product prices ($s - \gamma - \delta$)	0.11	0.06	0.11
Cost of capital (ρ)	0.10	0.10	0.10
Price of product $P(0)$ in €	800	800	1,000
Unit cost of production $C(0)$ in €	400	400	400
Quantities sold at $t = 0$	500,000	500,000	500,000
Rate of variation of sales φ_1	+0.08	+0.08	+0.08
Rate of variation of sales φ_2	+0.04	+0.04	+0.04
Rate of variation of sales φ_3	−0.10	−0.10	−0.10
Rate of variation of sales φ_4	−0.20	−0.20	−0.20
Tax rate adjusted	0.25	0.25	0.25
Total investment (€/mill.)	300	300	300
Value of the strategy (€/mill.)	−57	+114	+175
Product life T (years)	5	8	6

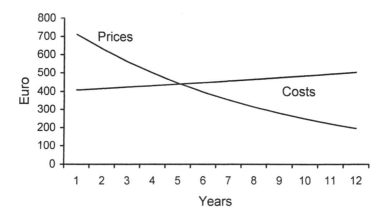

Figure 6.2   Dynamics of prices and costs (in €) of a new product: a simulation (case A)

All other assumptions remaining constant, the value of the strategy becomes positive and equals €114 million if the rate of price reduction for the product aging is 5%; in this case the life (*T*) of the new product rises to eight years (Case B). The value of the strategy is positive and equal to €175 million, if the competitive pressure reduces prices at 10% per year, but the launching price is equal to €1000 (Case C).

The simulation proves that the strategy value is very sensitive to the decreasing rate of price (*γ*), due to the competitive pressure of rivals' new products.

The success of the product innovation, expressed by the higher initial price, and the competitive pressure are, therefore, the main factors affecting the value of the strategy.

Table 6.1 shows the strategy values and the life of the new product with regard to the different hypotheses.

DOMINANT AND COLLATERAL STRATEGIES

The risk of an integrated strategy is the firm remaining 'stuck in the middle', as stated by Porter (1980). This occurs when the firm does not succeed in achieving the increments of productivity required to hold cost leadership; at the same time, it fails in clearly differentiating its own products from the rival ones.

In this way, the firm loses consumers demanding low price products, but also those prepared to pay higher prices for innovative and differentiated products. As Porter observes (1980) 'the firm stuck in the middle also probably suffers from a blurred corporate culture and a conflicting set of organizational arrangements and motivation system'.

This risk is real and it is necessary to avoid it. To this aim, the pursuit of a mixed strategy must not determine the loss of the firm's strategic identity, that is, its features, its specific way of being and operating in the competitive arena.[3]

For example, if the firm wants to remain being characterized as a competitor with high production differentiation, obtained by systematic innovation and constant attention to quality, it will adopt a strategy of product innovation as the dominant strategy of its development plan, even if it is pursuing a strategy of continuous increments in productivity. And vice versa.

In other words, pursuing a mixed strategy means matching the dominant strategy, that is that one which characterizes the development plan and on which the competitive advantage principally depends, with a collateral strategy. This is a support strategy, directed at realizing structural changes appropriate for holding the firm at least at the level of rivals, over the other variables characterizing its offer.

In the sectors considered, this firm development model is certainly complex; it requires a large and differentiated set of resources, a wide spectrum of management competencies and operating flexibility. And it is just this complexity that usually determines the so-called 'stuck in the middle' situations, at the origin of many firm crises. In the 1980s Chrysler, British Leyland and Fiat represented examples of stuck in the middle firms, with products not differentiated enough and product costs not sufficiently low to determine a competitive advantage over the rivals.

THE ALTERNATION OF DOMINANT INNOVATION STRATEGIES OVER A LONG PERIOD

In the long run the dynamics of environment and industry competition can make the adoption of different dominant strategies (productivity or product innovations) necessary, in various periods of a firm's life.

For example, in the consumer electronics industry, Matsushita has followed a typical strategy of cost leadership for many years, based on process and marketing innovations. After having gained a strong competitive advantage, the firm followed a strategy directed at consolidating its position for a long time, without venturing into product innovations. Instead, since the mid 1970s the firm has been obliged to modify its own strategy and to focus also on product innovation, because of the fast technical advances that have characterized the sector.

An opposite pattern has, on the other hand, been adopted by Sony. Due to strong competition, this firm has been obliged to devote itself to process innovation, in order to make up for loss of advantage over its rivals, after having adopted for a long period a strategy of strong product differentiation through an active policy of innovation and support of its image (Baba 1989).

These changes allowed the abovementioned firms to adapt the model of value creation to the new conditions occurring in the industry and in the market, because of technical advance and the appearance of new competitive forces.

Thus, the strategic identity too can be changed, but such changes require long time periods and high costs, so as to be able to adapt the capital of resources and competencies of the firm and modify the external firm image among the consumers. The analytical conditions for the two strategies creating value, when they are alternatively implemented, are not different from those described in the preceding chapters.

The difference to be underlined is the bigger risk for the firm, as a consequence of the supposed strategic change with respect to the pattern in progress. It involves the need for estimating a higher cost of capital with the consequent effects on the present value of cash flows.

The strategic change will determine, moreover, a higher investment of capital for the acquisition of the new resources and the training in the new competencies required.

STRATEGY FOCUS: INTEGRATED INNOVATION STRATEGIES IN SOME RELEVANT INDUSTRIES

Integrated Innovation Strategies in the Automotive Industry

In automotive industries, firms have been competing strongly through continuous product innovations. But also the increment of productivity has been an important factor in determining the competitive advantage of some firms. We have already cited the case of Toyota which based its extraordinary success on mixed product and productivity strategies.

Data shown in Table 6.2 give evidence of the difference in productivity increases between Japanese automotive firms and American ones (Lieberman, Lan and Williams 1990).

Table 6.2 *Increases in labour productivity in the automotive sector (average rates of change in percentage per year)*

	N cars/N employees			
	1950–60	1960–70	1970–80	1980–87
GM	−0.3	−0.3	2.2	0
Ford	0.3	−0.5	−1	7.6
Chrysler	0	−0.5	2.2	4.7
Toyota	22.3	9.5	4.7	−1.1
Nissan	20.1	9.4	4.4	−1.3
Mazda	NA	3	3.5/15.1*	3.4

	Added value/hours worked			
	1950–60	1960–70	1970–80	1980–87
GM	0.9	2.1	3.7	3.6
Ford	1.4	2.3	2.4	10
Chrysler	2.5	0.1	3	11.7
Toyota	NA	7.8	8.1	5.6
Nissan	NA	9.6	8.4	0.9
Mazda	NA	5.7	−0.1/15.5*	3.2

Note: * (1970–1975)/(1975–1980).

Source: Lieberman, Lan and Williams (1990).

This has certainly been an important factor of the exceptional expansion of some Japanese firms in the US market, in the 1950–1987 period.

Note that the significant productivity increment of Ford and Chrysler in the 1980s is due to the introduction of new productive and organizational techniques and to the production switch to cars of smaller dimension.

Integrated Innovation Strategies in the Microprocessor Industry

In the microprocessor industry, innovations in product and process are combined in an organic way, as a consequence of microelectronic development.[4]

Technology innovations have increased microprocessor performance, boosting the processing power, measured in millions of instructions per second (MIPS). This has been rising steadily, because of the increasing number of transistors on the chip.

In 1965, Intel co-founder Gordon Moore saw into the future. His prediction, now popularly known as Moore's Law, states that the number of transistors on a chip doubles about every two years. Through relentless pursuit of technology innovations this prediction has been confirmed after 40 years. Moore's Law also means decreasing costs. As silicon-based components and platform ingredients gain in performance, they become exponentially cheaper to produce and therefore more plentiful, more powerful, and more seamlessly integrated in the daily lives of customers. The exponential increases in the number of transistors integrated into a processor have steadily and reliably led to increasing performance, energy efficiency and capabilities in platforms and products.

Continuing to advance the process technology provides added benefits including less space per transistor, which enables putting more transistors on an equivalent size chip, and decreasing the size of the chip allows the industry to be able to offer an increased number of integrated features. These advancements have resulted in higher performing microprocessors, products that consume less power and/or products that cost less to manufacture.

Table 6.3 helps us understand the differences between the different processors introduced over the years. It refers to Intel production.[5] As you can see from this table, there is a relationship between clock speed and MIPS. The maximum clock speed is a function of the manufacturing process and delays within the chip. Modern processors can often execute at a rate of two instructions per clock cycle. That improvement is directly related to the number of transistors on the chip.

The effects of process innovations on costs reduction and product prices have been extraordinary. Obviously, to clearly evidence these effects, it is necessary to consider products at constant quality. To do this, some experts divide the cost and price of every microprocessor by the number of transistors that express the processing power.

According to recent research (Aizcorbe, Oliner and Sichel 2006), cost per transistor for frontier MPU (micro process unit) chips declined between 1995 and 2005 at an average annual rate of 34.7%.

Also prices declined between 1988 and 1994 at an average annual rate of −30%, between 1994 and 2001 at an average annual rate of −63.1% and between 2001 and 2004 at an average annual rate of −40.5 %.[6] See Figure 6.3.

All this clarifies the importance of continuous investments in new products and technologies for a firm wishing to continue operating in the sector and creating value.

Table 6.3   Advancing process technology and higher performing processors

Name	Date	Transistors (000)	Microns (1M=1000 nm)	Clock speed	Data width	MIPS
8080	1974	6	6	2 MHz	8 bits	0.64
8088	1979	29	3	5 MHz	16 bits 8-bit bus	0.33
80286	1982	134	1.05	6 MHz	16 bits	1
80386	1985	275	1.05	16 MHz	32 bits	5
80486	1989	1,200	1	25 MHz	32 bits	20
Pentium	1993	3,100	0.08	60 MHz	32 bits 64-bit bus	100
Pentium II	1997	7,500	0.35	233 MHz	32 bits 64-bit bus	~300
Pentium III	1999	9,500	0.25	450 MHz	32 bits 64-bit bus	~510
Pentium 4	2000	42,000	0.18	1.5 GHz	32 bits 64-bit bus	~1,700
Pentium 4 'Prescott'	2004	125,000	0.09	3.6 GHz	32 bits 64-bit bus	~7,000
Dual Core 2	2006	820,000	0.045	3,5 GHz	64-bit	

Source: Intel Annual Reports.

In this industry, Intel obtained the leadership through an integrated strategy of innovations in product and productive process. Intel was founded in 1968 and initially became a leader in the production of DRAM, SRAM and ROM memories, during the 1970s. In 1971, Marcian Hoff, Federico

Faggin, Stanley Mazor and Masatoshi Shima invented the first microprocessor, the Intel 4004. In 1982 Andy Grove abandoned the production of memories and concentrated activity on the microprocessor business. The firm rapidly developed in the 1980s through a sequence of new successful products and technologies. In 2006 Intel recorded $35.4 billion net revenues and $5.6 billion operating income; the firm has 94,100 employees throughout the world, 7,000 of which are researchers and scientists that work in R&D activities.

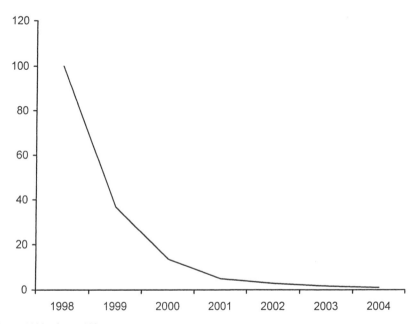

Note: 1998 price = 100.

Source: Author's elaboration on Aizcorbe, Oliner and Sichel (2006).

Figure 6.3   Price per transistor for frontier MPU chips

In the period 1971–2006, Intel introduced three radical innovations, the X80, X86 and Core architectures, and a high number of new types and models of each architecture, renewing them every two–three years (Table 6.4). For example, many processors are re-introduced at higher clock speeds for many years after the original release date.

In 2006 Intel introduced eight variants of its new product-architecture Dual Core onto the market, different in clock speed, front-side bus and cache memory, planning the renewal of them every two years. Intel also continues to invest in world-class technology development, particularly in the area of the design and manufacture of integrated circuits. Intel's CEO clearly defined the strategy:

> Our goal is to be the preeminent provider of semiconductor chips and platform solutions to the worldwide digital economy. As part of our overall strategy to compete in each relevant market segment, we use our core competencies in the design and manufacture of integrated circuits, as well as our financial resources, global presence, and brand recognition. Our strategy focuses on taking customer needs into account in developing the next generation of products and platforms that will enable new form factors and new usage models for businesses and consumers.

Process innovation is very important at Intel. This firm produces its microprocessors in its three 65-nanometre wafer fabrication facilities in Ireland, Arizona and Oregon and in two 90-nanometre wafer facilities in New Mexico and Ireland, being one year ahead of the rest of the technology industry. As of year-end 2006 the majority of microprocessors were manufactured on 300mm wafer fabrication facilities, using proprietary 65-nanometre process technology.

Each generation of process technology allows Intel to build products that cost less to manufacture, have improved performance and energy efficiency and offer more capabilities. For developing processors with improved performance, the firm has to synchronize the introduction of new micro-architecture with improvements in the silicon process technology.

To this aim, Intel has planned to introduce a new micro-architecture approximately every two years and ramp the next generation of silicon process technology in the intervening years. This coordinated schedule allows the firm to develop and introduce new products based on a common micro-architecture quickly, without waiting for the next generation of silicon process technology. To limit the risks of new technologies first the firm introduces the new production technology to an already tested architecture, then to the new architecture when a determined process gives good results and high returns.

At the end of 2006, Intel completed the development and scheduled to begin production on its next-generation 45-nanometre technology in the second half of 2007 and demonstrated five different 45-nanometre microprocessors for all major market segments.

Table 6.4 New architectures, models and processes at Intel

Year	Basic model	No. bit	Architecture generation	Production process technology	
				nanom.	wafer size
1971	8080	8	X80	10,000	na
1974	8085			6,000	
1978	8086	16	X86 I	3,000	na
1979	8088				
1980	80186				
1981	80188				
1982	80286		X86 II gen.	1,500	
1985	80386	32	X86 III gen.		
1988	80386 SL-EX		X86 IV gen.		
1989	80486			1,000	na
1993	PENTIUM	64	X86 V gen.	800	na
1995				600	
1996				350	
1997	PENTIUM II			250	
1998					
1999	PENTIUM III			180	
2000	PENTIUM IV				
2001				130	200mm
2002					
2003					
2004	PENTIUM IV			90	300mm
2005					
2006	CORE 2 DUO		CORE	65	300mm
2007				45	300mm

Notes:

(1) Transition from 200 mm wafer to 300 mm wafer provided more than twice as many equivalent chips per wafer.
(2) 1nm = 0.000,000,001 metre; there are 1 billion nanometres (nm) in one metre; 1 micron = 1000 nanometres.

Source: Intel annual reports and Intel website.

To advance in new products and in process technology, Intel invests a lot of money in R&D activities. Research and development expenditures in 2006 amounted to $5.9 billion ($5.1 billion in fiscal year 2005 and $4.8 billion in fiscal year 2004).

As can be seen from data shown in Table 6.5, R&D expenses increased from 8% of net revenues in 1995 to 16.7% in 2006. These increasing investments evidence the increasing effort to develop innovations for achieving new generations of platforms and products and at the same time for advancing in silicon manufacturing process technology.

The leadership in silicon technology enabled the firm to make Moore's Law a reality, doubling the density of transistors on integrated circuits about every two years.

Intel continues to invest in new manufacturing, packaging and testing processes as well as improving existing products and reducing costs.

Table 6.5   Net revenues and R&D expenses at Intel

Year	Net revenues ($ in billions)	R&D ($ in billions)	R&D/net revenues
1995	16.2	1.3	0.0802
1996	20.8	1.8	0.0865
1997	25.1	2.3	0.0916
1998	26.3	2.5	0.0951
1999	29.4	3.1	0.1054
2000	33.7	3.9	0.1157
2001	26.5	3.8	0.1434
2002	26.8	4.0	0.1493
2003	30.1	4.4	0.1462
2004	34.2	4.8	0.1404
2005	38.8	5.1	0.1314
2006	35.4	5.9	0.1667

Source: Intel Annual Reports.

Integrated Innovation Strategies in the Consumer Product Industry: the P&G Case

It is quite frequent in consumer product industries for firms to adopt mixed strategies of product and process innovation.

We cite the case of Procter & Gamble (P&G), a leading firm in some consumer industries, such as beauty and health, household care and others. P&G recorded $68 billion net sales in the fiscal year 2006. The company has an organizational structure that is made up of three Global Business Units (GBU) and a Global Operations group. The Global Operations group consists of the Market Development Organization (MDO) and Global Business Services (GBS).

The three Global Business Units are: Beauty and Health with $28.9 billion sales in 2006, Household Care with $33.5 billion sales, Gillette Blades and Razors with $6.4 billion sales.

Each GBU has the primary responsibility to develop the overall strategy, identifying common consumer needs and developing new product innovations and building brands through effective commercial innovations, marketing and sales.

Procter & Gamble markets products in nearly 50 categories, from laundry products and toothpaste to nappies and bone-disease therapies. The breadth of its business creates opportunities to connect technology across categories in unexpected ways. So the firm joins product innovation to process innovation.

P&G is deeply committed to innovation. The CEO recently said:

> innovation is our lifeblood – new ideas and new products that make consumers' lives better, build customer sales and profits and build P&G market share, sales, profits and total shareholder return.

To reach this aim, P&G has a global research and development organization, with more than 7,500 scientists working in 22 centres in 12 countries around the world. In 2004–2005, P&G invested $1.8 billion or 3.5% of net outside sales in R&D. This ranks the company as one of the top 20 largest R&D investors among US-based companies. And in fiscal year 2004–2005 P&G had 27,000 granted patents globally, with eight new patents each day.

At the same time that P&G has been investing in new products, it has also been investing in new technologies. Today, the company has more than 200 proprietary technologies in the market: in surface and phase chemistry, in control metal ions (e.g. calcium and sodium), in absorbent structure and materials, in production of perfumes, etc.

As results from statements in annual reports and empirical evidence show, this firm is committed to technological innovation and to a continued emphasis on superior products. P&G was a 1995 recipient of the National Medal of Technology, the highest award the US government gives for achievement in technology.

NOTES

1. There is a growing empirical evidence which supports the suitability of mixed or integrated strategies. On this subject, see also: Dess et al. (1995).
2. The condition $P(0) (1 + s - \gamma - \delta)^T = C(0)(1 + s)^T$ is equal to:

$$\left(\frac{1+s}{1+s-\gamma-\delta}\right)^T = \frac{P(0)}{C(0)}$$

Expressing this equation in logarithms with base $\alpha = (1 + s)/ (1+ s - \gamma - \delta)$ we have an equivalent equation that permits obtaining the variable T as:

$$T = \log_\alpha (P(0)/C(0)) = \log_\alpha e \log (P(0)/C(0)) = \frac{\log (P(0)/C(0))}{\log \alpha}$$

$$T = \frac{\log P(0) - \log C(0)}{\log(1+s) - \log(1+s-\gamma-\delta)}$$

3. The strategic identity is here defined on the basis of the prevailing (dominant) innovative strategy, represented by product innovations or by process innovations. Other authors, instead, use a multidimensional approach. For example Baba (1989), with reference to scale-intensive industries, makes the strategic identity dependent on a more complex set of features: 1) the willingness to risk; 2) the time of entering the new business; 3) the prevailing innovative strategy, innovation of product or process; 4) the model of entry on the market (broad front/specialization); 5) the strategic package adopted.
4. A microprocessor (chip), also called an integrated circuit, is a small thin piece of silicon into which the transistors making up the microprocessor have been etched. MIPS (millions of instructions per second) is a rough measure of the performance of a CPU and this depends on the number of transistors. So the improvement of MIPS is directly related to the number of transistors on the chip.
5. Data are compiled from The Intel Microprocessor Quick Reference Guide. The date is the year that the processor was first introduced. Many processors are re-introduced at higher clock speeds for many years after the original release date. Transistors is the number of transistors on the chip. You can see that the number of transistors on a single chip has risen steadily over the years. Microns is the width, in microns, of the smallest wire on the chip. For comparison, a human hair is 100 microns thick. As the feature size on the chip goes down, the number of transistors rises. Clock speed is the maximum rate that the chip can be clocked at. Clock speed will make more sense in the next section. Data Width is the width of the ALU. An 8-bit ALU can add/subtract/multiply/etc. two 8-bit numbers, while a 32-bit ALU can manipulate 32-bit numbers. An 8-bit ALU would have to execute four instructions to add two 32-bit numbers, while a 32-bit ALU can do it in one instruction. In many cases, the external data bus is the same width as the ALU, but not always. The 8088 had a 16-bit ALU and an 8-bit bus, while the modern Pentiums fetch data 64 bits at a time for their 32-bit ALUs. MIPS stands for 'millions of instructions per second' and is a rough measure of the

performance of a CPU. Modern CPUs can do so many different things that MIPS ratings lose a lot of their meaning, but you can get a general sense of the relative power of the CPUs from this column.
6. Using quality adjusted price indexes, Flamm (2003) estimated a decline of memory chip prices at a 37% average annual rate from 1975 to 1985 and at a 20% average annual rate from 1985 to 1996.

7. Designing the R&D system of innovation

INTRODUCTION AND OBJECTIVES

The implementation of innovation strategies requires the systematic accomplishment of R&D activities through specialized resources and structures. The innovation strategy allows the top management to define the resources and competences to be built and acquired for performing the R&D activities. These activities may be organized differently in relation to the characteristics of the firms, the nature of innovation processes and environment dynamics. Innovation achievement and success in terms of value growth depend largely on the effectiveness of organizational structures and, more generally, on the validity of the firm's management system.

In this chapter we define the criteria for designing the innovation development system of the firm. This depends primarily on the innovation strategy the management want to realize, considering the main environmental trends and the dynamics of competitive forces. The innovation strategy allows the innovation development cycle to be defined, as well as the characteristic activities to be carried out. We also analyse the organizational models for an effective innovation management, comparing the advantages and disadvantages of the integrated R&D activities, with respect to different outsourcing solutions.

INNOVATIONS AND R&D ACTIVITIES

Product and process innovations require the firm to carry out a systematic activity of research and development (R&D) through specialized structures. We mainly refer to innovations deriving from a formalized R&D activity, excluding therefore those innovations coming from different sources, such as design innovations and process innovations deriving from the adaptation and improvement of the production process with the same technology.[1]

In particular, R&D is activities through which the technical feasibility of new products and production processes are studied and experimented with and turned into a standardized and organized form that enables the industrial production to be at a low cost and of constant quality.

These R&D activities should be organized as a series of phases or stages through which, from the initial definition of project requisites and specifications, the prototypes and intermediate products are developed with increasing completion degree and functionality, until the new product for the market has been worked out (Dringoli 1989 and 2006). These phases, in order of succession, identify the innovation development cycle. The innovation development cycle will clearly differ from project to project, in terms of both required activities and accomplishment time.

In the various phases of the cycle, which can be further broken down in relation to the complexity of the project, the inputs and outputs of the research and development activities (labour, machinery, equipment and various tools) will be different, in relation to the typical technology of the operating phase and the required resources.

However, the common element characterizing R&D activities is uncertainty regarding both the output (characteristics) and its completion time, and the quantity of necessary resources (inputs).

More precisely, uncertainty concerns both the technical characteristics of the project (technical or internal uncertainty), such as for example reliability, resistance, weight, dimension, etc., and the commercial value of the new product, as far as acceptance degree on the market is concerned (commercial or external uncertainty).

The innovative process, therefore, can be considered as a collection of interrelated activities, some directed at solving problems and eliminating the uncertainty of the project, others directed at the working out of prototypes and setting up of equipment (activities of engineering routine) (Table 7.1). These activities specify the type and the quantities of resources and competences necessary for their completion.

While the project shows a high variability of results in the initial phase, due to the high technical and commercial uncertainty, this variability tends to shrink progressively, as long as the development proceeds, up to the production set-off.

Naturally, as long as the innovation development cycle proceeds, the progressive reduction of uncertainty increases the causal comprehension (relationship between cause and effect), but also increases the imitation capabilities of competitors.

Regarding the time required to complete the innovative cycle, obviously it differs from product to product with respect to the phases constituting the cycle. In general, it is particularly high for the settlement stage of prototypes and pilot plants (with variable percentages between 40% and 50%) and for the stage of production set-off and building up of production capacities (from 20% to 30%).

Table 7.1   The stages of the innovation development cycle and the characteristic activities

Stages of innovation process	Activities directed to resolution of uncertainties	Engineering routine activities
Stage 1		
Definition of project requisites and basic specifics *Output: basic project specifics*	Studies, experiences, expert consultancies, coordination with marketing staff	Writing up of projects, conformity check of standards and compatibility with other products, etc.
Stage 2		
Project of prototype or pilot plant, building up, various links and tests *Output: prototype or pilot plant*	Analysis, model construction, solution of technological problems, tests on materials and models or on prototypes	Realization of design and technical drafts of prototypes and pilot plant and their components
Stage 3		
Setting up of equipment, markets evaluation, production planning *Output: new product*	Studies for markets evaluation, analysis of plant alternatives; market test on product, etc.	Preparation of detailed designs for the equipment needed for the organization of production; choice of product components to be found outside the firm, etc.
Stage 4		
Construction and installation of production equipment; start of production		Personnel training; setting up of equipment and production procedures; definition of specifics of semi-finished products and purchases in general.

For example, in the pharmaceutical sector, the development cycle of a new drug, with particular reference to a research paradigm based on the chemical synthesis, is characterized by a high number of phases, of very long length, and has results which are highly uncertain. The entire process of research and development of a new drug, as a new chemical entity (NCE), lasts on average 14 years; while the development cycle of new drugs, such as new compounds or dosages, is far shorter, etc.[2]

The complexity of R&D activities, lengths of accomplishment and uncertainty of results will depend on the innovation strategy, that is the technology relative to the new product and the intensity of the innovation pursued (Table 7.2).

Table 7.2   Types of innovation and uncertainty level

Innovation types	Uncertainty
Radical product and process innovations accomplished outside the firm	Very high uncertainty
Important and radical product innovations accomplished inside the firm	High uncertainty
New generations of existing products	Moderate uncertainty
Imitations of new products or modifications of existing products and processes	Low uncertainty
New models, product differentiation, technical improvements, etc.	Very low uncertainty

Source: Author's elaboration from Freeman (1974).

Innovations of models of products generally show low uncertainty levels in both expected results and time of accomplishment and require limited capital investment. They are incremental innovations, necessary for the firm to keep up with competitors, to 'update' its offerings along with market needs and changes, or to reduce production costs.

These innovations mainly consist in the empowerment of product performances, refining or improvement of processes with a given technology, etc. They consist in new types and models that achieve more or less significant improvements of existing products – new products obtained through the same basic technology with similar destinations and belonging to the same category or species of products. These are, for example in the pharmaceutical field, new dosage and packaging formulas of products (tablets, liquid, etc.), or composite products produced by combining together already existing chemical entities. In the automobile industry these innovations are represented by new car models or types, etc.

In general, these innovations are the result of both the operating activity in production and marketing, and the R&D activity.

Radical innovations of products and processes are, on the contrary, changes involving discontinuities with the technological heritage and already known markets, so as to cause breakthrough effects on the existing products and technologies.

They show higher uncertainty in both the technical outcomes and the possible market results, and require in general high investments in both R&D activities and new production structures. In the case of product innovations, they are new products or specialities previously unknown, which satisfy latent needs or solve previously unsatisfied needs in a radical way. Examples in the pharmaceutical field are the new drugs such as cortisone, the Sabin vaccine and Viagra; in the chemical industry they are products such as nylon, polyethylene, etc.

THE SYSTEM OF INNOVATION DEVELOPMENT: FUNDAMENTAL COMPONENTS AND CHARACTERISTICS

In order to systematically accomplish R&D activities, more or less complex structures are required which are sufficiently autonomous but adequately linked to the operating activities of the firm (production, marketing, logistics, etc.).

On the whole, they configure the firm system of innovation development or the system of technological development, such as a firm sub-system specialized for the systematic production of innovations through the use of ad hoc resources and competences.[3]

Among the components of this system, the personnel represents the main resource. In general, it is characterized by higher education and special degree (technicians, engineers, computer engineers, biologists, chemists, etc.) compared with those of other firm sub-systems. The other fundamental component of the system is given by machinery, plant and analysis and research equipment, often of a high technological level.

The output of the innovation system is represented by new products and processes, registered patents and registration in progress patents (Figure 7.1). In industries where the technical progress and the change of consumer tastes and behaviours are incessant and fast, the system of innovation development is the core of the firm; it is the real producer of the firm change.

Emblematic is the case of pharmaceutical companies, where product innovation, based on systematic R&D activity, is absolutely relevant in the competitive contest within the industry and greatly influences the turnover and the profitability of the firm.

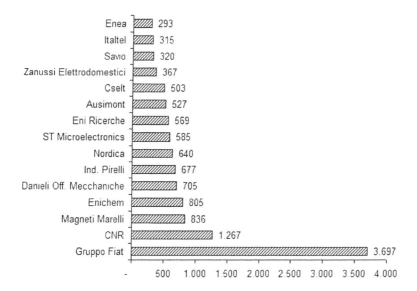

Source: *Il Sole 24 Ore*, 29.10.2006.

Figure 7.1   Number of requests for patents presented in 2005 in Europe

The system of innovation development, even if autonomous from the operating firm's sub-system, must be opportunely coordinated with it, that is with the activities concerning production, sales and distribution of products.

Autonomy is needed to use the existing resources as is best possible and promote the development of innovations in directions enabling the maximization of the business value (Martins and Terblanche 2003; Munari and Sobrero 2004).

The relevant characteristics of an innovation development system are:

- dimension;
- flexibility;
- integration degree of R&D activities.

Regarding the dimension, this is represented by the amount of employed resources: number of workers and invested capital in R&D activities. The flexibility of the system is expressed by the variety and the rapidity of innovative processes the system is capable of developing. The degree of integration of R&D activities is the level of R&D activities the firm carries out internally for producing innovations. The firm can be organized to perform the entire innovation cycle directly, from the basic research activities to the applied ones and the product development, or otherwise it may only perform some phases of the cycle, externalizing the others.[4]

THE DESIGN OF THE INNOVATION DEVELOPMENT SYSTEM: PLANNING R&D RESOURCES AND COMPETENCES

Designing the innovation development system of a firm requires specifying its relevant characteristics, that is: dimension; flexibility degree; integration degree of R&D activities.

As far as dimension is concerned, this decision requires estimating the needs of resources (personnel, machinery, plant, etc.) for developing innovation in the different stages of the cycle, considering the industry the firm operates in and the intensity of pursued innovation.

Regarding the flexibility of the system, this decision will influence the characteristics of the personnel, in terms of professional knowledge and versatility of researchers and the specialist degree of R&D machinery and equipment. This is a fundamental feature for the survival and the success of the firm, since the technological changes can be sudden and unexpected and the firm has to be able to promptly respond to the changes of consumer preferences and market policies of competitors.

Finally, regarding the degree of integration of R&D activities, it is a matter of defining the level of participation of the firm in the production of innovations, through directly managed R&D structures.

The different solutions have a great influence upon the quality and the levels of resources needed for the R&D, in personnel and equipment, and therefore have different costs. In some sectors, the amount of resources required to accomplish the whole R&D allows only larger companies to have the structures to develop the entire innovation process autonomously.

To have an idea of the dimension and of the complexity the system of technological development can assume in some big companies, consider the data shown in Table 7.3 on the R&D expenditure of the top five international companies by business.

The decision concerning the characteristics of the innovation development system (dimension, flexibility and integration degree) requires the management to carefully evaluate the following:

- R&D technologies and their dynamics in the industry;
- the characteristics of the firm: resources and competences in R&D, dimension, financial capacity, etc.

Technologies and their dynamics in the industry will influence the basic characteristics of the innovation system of the firm. In particular, they will influence the dimension of this system (Table 7.3).

Table 7.3   *R&D expenses of top five international companies by sector (data in million $, year 2000)*

Electronics		TLC equipment		Automotive		Aerospace/ defence		Pharmaceutical	
IBM	5,129	Ericsson	4,446	Ford	7,400	Boeing	1,936	Pfizer	4,847
Matsu-shita	5,016	Lucent	3,986	GM	6,600	Un.Tech.	1,254	Glaxo-SK	3,702
NEC	3,052	Nortel	3,986	Daimler-Ch	5,348	EADS	1,139	Johnson & J	3,600
Fujitsu	3,038	Cisco S	3,432	Toyota	3,674	Honeywell	0.780	Merck	2,456
HP	2,646	Nokia	2,465	Volkswagen	3,022	Rayteon	0.475	Bristol-Meyer	2,350

Source: Guerci (2002).

Think of the big R&D structures of firms operating in the so-called science-based sectors, that is in sectors such as net producers of technologies (Pavitt 1984).

In these businesses, the firms get the technological opportunities and the specific knowledge from the scientific research or basic research; therefore they need complex laboratory structures and great investment in R&D. In the group of science-based sectors there are the aerospace, the precision mechanics and scientific equipment and a great part of the fine chemical and pharmaceutical industries (except fine chemicals destined for consumption such as cosmetics, detergents, etc.), as well as a great part of electronics (except for so-called consumption electronics).

Moreover, R&D activity is relevant in the so-called scale-intensive sectors, such as automobiles, appliances, consumption electronics, etc. Even if these firms realize production dominated by assembling and transformation processes on a large scale, widely devoted to technological improvement coming from upward sectors, they deal directly with product innovation accomplished through continuous technical, performance, reliability and consumption improvements.

Conversely, the innovation development system has a minor dimension, in terms of involved resources, in the traditional sectors such as clothing, furniture, the shoe business, etc. (Table 7.4).

Table 7.4 The different intensity of R&D activities in various industrial sectors

Sectors	Intensity of R&D	R&D/ turnover
Shoe, textile, clothing	Low	Less than 3%
Automobile, consumption electronics	Medium	From 3% to 10%
Computer, aeronautical, pharmaceutical	High	Greater than 10%

Source: Piccaluga (1996).

In these sectors the innovation is mainly linked to design rather than technical progress and only some leading firms have laboratory R&D and evolved technical offices. However, the absence of research laboratories or other departments specialized in innovation production does not mean that the firm does not participate in the development and technical change in general. Firms use patents and the know-how of other firms and perform internal development activities useful for the transfer and acquisition of new knowledge.

The characteristics of the firm represent the second variable influencing the architecture of the innovation development system. In particular, the endowment of resources and competences in R&D becomes fundamental for the configuration of the system. They mainly influence the flexibility and integration degree of the R&D system. When the management of the entire innovation process, from the first research phases to the commercialization of the new product, requires knowledge and competence resources that the firm does not possess in the quantities and varieties required, it is better to externalize activities requiring non-available resources and competences.[5]

Based on this general criterion, the vertical integration degree of the innovation process will be defined, as well as the possible recourse to alliances and joint ventures. In particular, the recourse to strategic alliances and the building up of joint ventures will represent solutions enabling the use of complementary resources external to the firm's boundaries, or the joining of necessary resources to complete the innovation process, or taking the innovation to the market, or sharing the investment risk. In the pharmaceutical and electronics sectors, for example, these solutions are widespread; also large firms such as Merck, Sony, General Electric and IBM have set up joint ventures, strategic alliances and external supply agreements, when they have realized the need to use capabilities and competences external to their boundaries (Grant 1998).

The characteristics of the innovation development system will depend, furthermore, on the dimension of the firm. Innovation is a costly process in both production and accomplishment; this means it is necessary to organize R&D so that the costs are not excessive in relation to the expected benefits coming from new products in the time of innovation exploitation.

In general a larger firm has a greater capacity to sustain the costs and risks associated with R&D activities. This is confirmed by the empirical evidence which shows that only a limited number of minor firms systematically carry out R&D activities. On the other hand, the majority of larger firms have a real, variably articulated, innovation development system.

According to some researchers (Bonaccorsi 2001; Sobrero 2001) only a smaller number of small and medium enterprises (1–3%) develop new technologies and show consistent resources dedicated to R&D activities, with an incidence of R&D expenses on their turnover higher than that of larger firms. A greater number of small and medium enterprises, approximately 10–15%, seem to be advanced users of technology, with formalized R&D structures, evolved labs and technical offices.

The greater presence of R&D activities in larger firms is confirmed by recent studies conducted in Italy on firms with more than 20 employees (Macioce 2001). Factors impeding the innovation activities are mainly represented by too high innovation costs, perception of an excessive economic risk and lack of financial resources and qualified personnel (Table 7.5).

Based on the abovementioned research, it turns out that the nature of innovation activities seems also to be linked to the size of the firm. The smaller firms base their innovation activity mainly on the external acquisition of technical progress through the purchase of machinery and services, while the firms with more than 1,000 employees base their innovation activity mainly on R&D activity.[6]

Table 7.5 Firms which have introduced innovations in 1994–96 in Italy (by firm dimension)

No. of employees	Firms with systematic R&D (in % of their category)
20–49	7.3
50–99	18.2
100–249	27.0
250–499	43.3
500–999	54.1
1,000 and over	72.4
Total (average)	12.5

Source: Macioce (2001).

THE ADVANTAGES OF AN INTEGRATED R&D SYSTEM

In industries characterized by process firms, such as the chemical and pharmaceutical industries, the innovation development system is usually organized inside the firm, according to a linear scheme with an ordered sequence of operations, where the output of each phase represents the input of the following one, until the accomplishment of the innovation. The entire cycle is mainly performed inside the firm, where both the applied research and the development are conducted, with the intervention of specialists belonging to different disciplines. From the first formulation, the new product is progressively worked out through various experimentation phases, until the production industrialization stage and the start-up of the production process on an industrial scale.

A different organizational model provides the parallel aligning of some phases of the product development; where, in general, the initial pre-study and feasibility are performed in sequence, the other phases are performed with a partial overlapping.

These are organizational solutions inspired by the principle of 'concurrent engineering', according to which some phases of the development process are developed in parallel alignment and temporal overlapping, with the exchange of preliminary information between upstream and downstream activities.

This overlapping provides the advantage of a reduction of the innovation lead time, but the uncertainty of results increases, because of the interdependence between different phases (Stalk and Hout 1990; Clark and Fujimoto 1991; Sobrero 1999; Munari and Sobrero 2004).

A firm has an advantage in pursuing an integrated R&D activity (in-house), when it already has the required resources, capabilities and competences. The advantages coming from performing R&D activities directly may be summarized as follows.

- *Better understanding of research and innovation processes*: in-house research is essential for starting one's own technological innovation projects, as well as for understanding research performed by others, either firms or research centres. This is more important when a firm has to assimilate or rapidly recombine outside produced knowledge of various types or to acquire technological competences from external sources. The capability for identifying interactions between new research activities and existing products and production systems requires the availability of specialized researchers, possessing a wider viewpoint (Iansiti 1993).
- *Exploitation of spin-off*: internal R&D activity is important in order to exploit knowledge developed in other application fields and to benefit from the positive effects of non-visible and not easily evaluated outcomes (Cohen and Levinthal 1990).
- *Protection against opportunistic behaviour*: a research project often represents a starting point for further research, so the firm is vulnerable to the opportunistic behaviour of other firms taking part in an agreement. In general, the final development phases of a new product provide greater possibilities of defence against opportunistic behaviour.[7]
- *Avoidance of transfer difficulties*: practical difficulties in transferring technological and managerial competences from the outside to the inside of firms favour the reinforcement of in-house research activities.
- *Imperfection of knowledge resource markets*: in the case of R&D, the new knowledge resources are tacit and not codified and the final outcome is unforeseeable by definition.[8] In these markets property rights become vague and the evaluation of resources is complex. Consequently, the purchasing of technological resources through the market exposes the firm to high risks of predatory behaviour, for the impossibility of correctly valuating and monitoring the activities of suppliers. Since a market of knowledge resources is hard to establish and sustain over time, firms tend either to maintain their R&D activities inside or to search for collaboration agreements.

Summarizing, the integration of innovation activities is favoured by high transaction costs, relative to the intermediate outputs, preventing the efficient functioning of supply markets of products and services.

We refer to the costs and risks of contractual forms for structuring the relationship, ex-ante defining the objectives of collaboration, its control, the distribution of costs and results, the means of access, exchange and protection of proprietary technologies, monitoring and ex-post control of agreements and attainment of established goals. Further difficulties derive, in addition, from the need for specific investments dedicated to the relationship and the resulting long-term duties.

In some cases, the firm gains a greater advantage by breaking down the R&D, creating new specialized firms (spin-offs), with highly qualified professionals, to manage the activity of R&D of new projects. These new projects show minor strategic relevance and a lower affinity with the firm core business, but are anyway important. The benefit of such a solution is the possibility to better exploit competences that could not be adequately exploited in the firm of origin because of organizational limits. Enucleating and transferring outside some phases of the innovation process into a new autonomous firm may enable an enlargement of the potential market and move the efficiency edge forward. In particular, this solution allows the exploitation of innovative and excess knowledge that the firm produces but is not able to exploit fully, due to the routine rigidity or the presence of bonds of incompatibility with pre-existing activities.

THE ADVANTAGES OF A DECENTRALIZED R&D SYSTEM

Collaborating with other firms can be an extraordinary tool for extending the knowledge range, exploiting complementary resources and building up the foundations for obtaining easier access to new markets (Norman and Ramirez 1994; Lorenzoni 1992).

This is true especially when the resources and competences relevant for the generation and commercial exploitation of new products and production processes are only partially present inside the firm.

Furthermore, thanks to collaboration, the firm has the possibility to share part of the R&D costs. This is particularly relevant in sectors where the change of technologies is very rapid and requires both large financial resources and high technical capabilities a single firm does not always have (Kotable and Swan 1995). Obviously, there is also the other side of the coin: profits must be shared with the partner and there is the risk that the transferred know-how might be used in the future by the partner for competing against the firm.

Cooperation with other firms in R&D activities can assume the form of temporary partnerships, limited to particular projects, or the form of real alliance, that is an extended and long-term partnership.

Once the strategic relevance of the collaboration has been defined, it is necessary to define the distribution of rights among the partners and choose the legal government form. Finally, it is necessary to define the most adequate organizational form, with regard to partners' resources and the operating modes of coordination and integration of activities.

Considering the contractual form and the interdependence degree of resources, it is possible to classify agreements and alliances in the following types (Sobrero 1999):[9]

- *Joint ventures:* firms involved in the alliance opt for the combination of their own resources in an autonomous company;
- *Investment of risk capital:* purchase or exchange of minority stock shares;
- *Client/supplier agreements:* collaborations regulated by a contract for the development of a new product or a new production process or a phase of this.

Regarding joint ventures, they are a particular type of strategic alliance in which two or more firms interested in the accomplishment of the same project provide capital and resources useful for the accomplishment of the product to a new independent organization, controlling its management.

In this case, there is a joint involvement of partners in the juridical and formal control of the collaboration initiative, through the creation of a third company, distinct from the partners, in which they retain a capital share. This new juridical entity has as its specific objective the object itself of the collaboration, which might be the accomplishment of a project, the development of a particular product, or the commercialization of a technology in a given geographical area.

Often joint ventures involve two firms, one small but endowed with particularly innovative technological resources, and a larger firm, with a high market position and resources and competences needed to define and create a commercial plan for the launch of the new product.

The joint venture provides different benefits of an economic and organizational kind. First of all, it integrates the distinctive resources and capabilities of partners; second, it lets the firm rapidly enter a new business through agreement with a firm already operating in it. Compared with the internal development, the joint venture enables a more rapid entrance into new businesses.

Managing a joint venture is, however, technically difficult. Occasions for conflict between partners are in fact numerous and, in the initial phase, disparities of point of view regarding the investment plan frequently emerge, as well as disparities about the evaluation techniques of results. Some of these disparities can be solved during the negotiation before the agreement, but it is harder to manage conflicts emerging subsequently over unexpected facts. In addition, the balance between what a partner provides to the joint venture and what he gets back does not last long; due to this, the request to renegotiate the agreement on new bases follows (Harrigan 1986).

Particularly interesting are, in some sectors, the ability of medium and large firms to obtain resources and competences possessed by small or recently constituted enterprises that are considered important for covering some specific internal gaps. The objective is the creation of a strategic partnership through the acquisition of a minority share, with a possible option to increase it in the following period.

In general, the search for small dynamic and innovative organizations is spurred on by the difficulties faced by larger organizations to proceed rapidly to a turnaround of internal resources for matching radical changes in the competitive environment.[10]

Summarizing, from a strategic point of view, conditions determining the advantage of joint R&D activities are the following.

- *The progressive increase of resources* needed for bringing a new idea to commercial success favours collaboration among firms; these dynamics are particularly evident in a sector such as the pharmaceutical one, where in the last thirty years we have witnessed a significant increase in costs sustained for the development of new drugs.
- *Scope economies*: the cost benefits of collaboration derive from the possibility to pursue multi-product and multi-market strategies, thanks to investment dedicated to distinctive technological competence.
- *Risk sharing*: there are advantages in collaboration also in terms of risk reduction for the single firm; they emerge through the distribution of invested capital on multiple innovation projects.
- *Enlargement of internal resource and competence base*: collaboration and alliances represent in many cases a strategic way to access intangible resources, such as know-how and technical competences the firm does not possess. Collaboration, in fact, enables the firm to open a 'technological window' accessing different markets and businesses from those it presently dominates.

Regarding the client/supplier agreements, these are forms of collaboration that have been increasing dramatically over the last decade.[11]

This organizational choice generally allows the firm to have low costs and quick responding structures. That is due to the higher agility of specialized external firms compared to the internal R&D structures of the firm and the higher incentives offered to the personnel, particularly bonuses such as stock options and other benefits (Chesbrough and Teece 2002).

A very interesting example is offered by Procter & Gamble. This firm up until the late 1980s had a centralized R&D structure that numbered around 7,500 employees; it then moved to a hybrid R&D model with a growing recourse to small and medium external firms. In 2001 around 15% of new products launched were developed outside the firm and in 2006 around 35% of new products incorporated elements designed outside. It should also be noted that in the period 2003–2005 the firm launched more than 100 products on the market; in this period the success rate of products more than doubled and innovation costs were drastically reduced. The investment in R&D, measured as a percentage of total revenues, went down from 4.8% in 2000 to 3.4% in 2006. In particular, those activities performed outside the firm in a more efficient way have been externalized, concentrating internal activities in those areas where the firm had distinctive competencies that could not be easily reproduced outside.

The pharmaceutical industry is another sector where in the last ten years a surge in the outsourcing of R&D activities has been developing, because of the pressure of new technologies, the complexity and variety of new knowledge and the dramatic increase in costs and risks of innovation. At present, in this sector the R&D is not an activity centralized in single firms, but a decentralized system of activities, articulated in complex nets of agreements and alliances between firms, binding together synergic assets and resources.[12]

The general factors pushing firms to R&D outsourcing are the following.

- *High uncertainty of output and necessity of flexibility.* Outsourcing R&D activities allows the firm to avoid the costs of hiring, training and maintaining over time a staff of researchers that will have to be enlarged as soon as its competencies are insufficient to allow competitiveness. The decision to externalize R&D activities has the positive effect of turning the fixed costs related to the maintenance of a research laboratory (that is concentrated in a particular area and that has certain competencies) into variable costs to be sustained only when specific competencies in certain fields of research are needed. Also, dropping a research project that has been externalized is quicker and cheaper than dropping an internally developed project. In particular the firm will not have to afford the greatest part of the unavoidable sunk costs connected to a research activity carried out in-house.

- *Cost reduction through concentration on key processes.* Outsourcing non-critical and routine R&D activities to specialized providers allows the firm to focus on key areas of its research and to strengthen its competencies. The better resource allocation raises the efficiency and therefore reduces costs. Sometimes, firms prefer to start partnerships to perform some phases of innovation development. An example of that is the participation of suppliers in the design phase, quite common especially within firms that produce complex goods. Suppliers can also be required to take part in co-design projects for components and sub-systems. In these cases the decentralization of design activities to suppliers reduces the amount of work of engineers and designers inside the firm and helps in focusing on tasks that can be better performed with the firm's competencies, with relevant benefits in terms of risk and cost reduction.

- *Access to knowledge resources, competencies and technologies not owned.* Innovation in many fields more frequently has a systemic characteristic and is based on interdisciplinary competencies that, in general, single firms cannot develop and control entirely inside their structures. Outsourcing R&D activities enables reducing the know-how gap in areas where the firm does not have experience or is not undertaking research. Very often the gap to be closed lies in innovative or specialist competence areas. In such cases an outsourcing strategy allows the firm to: a) avoid the expenses for the acquisition of technologies and know-how; b) get quick access to research facilities without having to create them; c) reduce the time needed to acquire and install technologies; d) avoid investments in training for its staff of researchers. Outsourcing some research activities can facilitate the process of reorganization of the entire research division, focusing internal activities on critical competences and giving the firm more time to learn new research methodologies, with the objective of internalizing the most fruitful.

- *Opening a 'window' on new technologies.* No firm, no matter how big, can make progress in all fields of research. Outsourcing gives an insight into the evolution of research in various fields, offering the possibility of exploiting the results obtained in external laboratories more quickly and more effectively. It is a tool for exploring new fields in technology, without being forced to employ, train and maintain a large R&D team.

The main disadvantages of outsourcing R&D can be summed up as follows.

- *Risk of loss of critical competencies and supplier dependency.* Outsourcing R&D activities can make the firm dependent on its specialized suppliers ('hold up' risk). In particular, the practice of contracting out relevant parts of the R&D process to the same provider for a long period of time makes the firm more vulnerable and implies a risk of loss of control on some research activities. In the future the firm could be damaged by the lack of direct experience, or by the difficulty of learning from external sources. Transferring research activities to external agents, the firm could have difficulties in establishing its own knowledge network and acquiring new competencies or introducing itself with a sound reputation into new markets. So it may be better keeping in-house R&D on crucial components, those having a substantial influence on the products' costs and quality. In any case it is necessary for the firm to keep a strong grasp on the knowledge necessary for the development and integration of the business system.
- *Absence of a shared vision and conflict of interests.* Interest conflicts often arise between the parts, due to the absence of a shared view and converging objectives (Chesbrough and Teece 2002). One of the main reasons why interest conflicts arise is the multi-client strategy of the supplier, sometimes in competition with the client firm. This obviously creates a risk of technology transfer through the provider.
- *Possibility of creating new competitors.* The creation of external competences increases the risk that they can be used in the future by the research provider for competing activities. This risk is high when the link with the supplier performing R&D activities implies the transfer of product- or process-related technologies.
- *Difficulty of measuring and evaluating the performance of a research supplier.* In order to evaluate the performance of external firms in carrying out the R&D activities, a firm should maintain a good knowledge of the ongoing research. That can be both difficult and complex, in particular when managing and controlling a large portfolio of research. An effective monitoring system can require large financial resources and strong competencies for assuring the activities carried out by the provider comply with the firm's standards and objectives.
- *Difficulty in coordinating activities related to the outsourcing strategy.* This strategy requires great competence in formulating contracts and handling relationships with partners. So, it is crucial to keep an open

mind in order to avoid the not-invented-here syndrome, a very common condition in many R&D departments of firms carrying out the process of developing innovation internally. Furthermore, in the case of outsourcing some problems in communication may arise and thus delays and misunderstandings. These problems can be more serious when the partners do not know each other very well and a relation based on trust does not yet exist.

INTERNALIZING AND DECENTRALIZING THE R&D ACTIVITIES AS COMPLEMENTARY SOLUTIONS

The decision to acquire R&D externally will be advantageous, when a firm with settled technological assets is faced with wide technological changes that concern the firm competencies.[13] In these cases the strategic choice to resort to external sources of resources and technological competencies allows the knowledge available to the firm to be extended and therefore fuels the dynamic process of creating new knowledge and integrating that into the technological competencies of the firm.

The outsourcing of some R&D phases will make the organizational structure much more flexible and the process control easier. But this decision also influences the firm's process of knowledge accumulation, which over time defines the strategic assets owned by the firm. So in some cases internalizing the R&D activities is preferred.

However, it is more and more difficult to consider R&D externalization and, in a wider sense, the acquisition of external know-how as an alternative strategy to the development of innovative capacities inside the firm.

Very often (e.g. in pharmaceutical research) it has been demonstrated that the sources of success, determined by the innovation performance of the firm, were to be found not only in the in-house development capacities, but mostly in the capacity of acquiring complementary technology and information from outside.

In many industries the two solutions appear to be complementary, since the capacity to undertake internal research is a necessary condition for fully exploiting the externally acquired knowledge. A solid knowledge of R&D activities is a necessary requisite for giving the organization the skills for learning and improving the externally acquired knowledge (Cohen and Levinthal 1990). More and more firms create modern systems to perceive technical opportunities from outside and hire managers of knowledge channels.

Moreover the decision to invest in R&D directly should not be considered an irreversible decision. Over time it is influenced by the nature of technology, competencies, innovation capacities and the firm experience. Different technologies have different evolutionary trajectories and have different degrees of uncertainty and speed of change.

ORGANIZATIONAL MODELS OF R&D ACTIVITIES

The Fundamental Objectives to Achieve: Creativity and Efficiency

Organizing innovative processes not only means defining the characteristics of the innovation system, but also creating an appropriate structure for promoting, realizing and monitoring R&D activity according to scheduled objectives.

This also requires the assessment of necessary competencies to be created and acquired, considering the external sources (e.g. universities and research laboratories) and the opportunities of cooperation with other firms.

To this aim it is necessary to remember that a part of knowledge is codified and then it can be transmitted among the firms; but a large part of knowledge useful for the innovation is tacit, idiosyncratic and strictly bound to the organization that generated it and so it is difficult to transfer and imitate (Malerba 1992; Grant 1998).

The organizational structure for managing R&D activities has to be designed so that processes of knowledge communication and development can be supported, as well as the building up of new knowledge and competences. Above all, the organizational architecture must stimulate creativity. The choice regarding the organizational structure of R&D is very important, because it determines the operational conditions in which the activities are carried out and the effectiveness of the innovation system.

The solutions the firm can adopt are different according to the innovation strategies, the necessary resources, and the complexity of the R&D activities to be carried out. In particular, the organizational structure of the R&D activities must be designed to deal with two fundamental but different objectives. On one hand it has to provide the technological competencies specific for the field of research in which the firm has decided to work, coordinating them and addressing them to reach the objectives of the innovative processes. On the other hand the R&D structure has to provide every project with the necessary information, knowledge and technical equipment so that it may advance through the various steps of development until completion.

Different organizational structures through which the system of innovation development is handled are the result of the need to satisfy the two contrasting objectives hereby presented in different ways.

The most frequently used structures for R&D activities are the following (Daft 2001; Munari and Sobrero 2004):

- *functional structures*; characterized by an innovation system divided into units specialized in certain functional areas (specialized disciplines or phases of the process);
- *product lines structures*; characterized by an innovation system divided into units linked to certain products or lines of products;
- *project structures*; characterized by an innovation system divided into units specialized in research projects;
- *matrix structures*; characterized by an innovation system divided into units specialized in functional areas (specialized disciplines) and in research projects.

Some firms present hybrid organizational frames to adequately solve development and monitoring problems connected to the various ongoing innovative processes.

Hybrid organizational structures can be found in the pharmaceutical sector, in which technological innovation and especially product innovation is crucial. In this sector it is not uncommon to find multinational firms working on various areas of medicine (products) and at all the stages of the innovation cycle. They present complex matrix structures, capable of coping with the research needs of the different lines of the product, dealing with various scientific disciplines in the same innovative process, characterized by different phases in terms of uncertainty and temporal horizon.

Functional Structure

The functional structure is characterized by the aggregation in the same organizational unit (e.g. a department, a laboratory and so on) of all the necessary resources (e.g. researchers, technicians, specialists, equipment and lab instruments) for the activities dealing with the same research discipline or the same technique (making physicians work with physicians only, biologists with biologists only and so on). Thus, each research area has its own group of specialists, only working in that area.

In other words, the R&D activity is divided according to the scientific fields necessary for carrying out the project and the innovation system is split into departments and laboratories specialized in different disciplines. According to this criterion, specialists and equipment are grouped together under the direction of a functional manager. Thus, the project is divided into sub-projects assigned to different departments and within each department to a specific laboratory and/or group of researchers. The director of each department coordinates internal activities and is in charge of the advancement of the project. The R&D director supervises and controls the functional departments.

For example, if we assume the R&D activities for a new medicine require knowledge in biology, pharmacology, chemistry and toxicology, the innovation system of the firm will be made up of a chemistry department, a pharmacology department, and so on, with specialists in each of these disciplines. In this way each field of research is taken care of by a team of experts grouped together and supplied with the necessary equipment; each area is vertically connected to the top, so that the general manager of research can supervise and monitor each specialist function (Figure 7.2).

The functional structure is the organizational structure historically used in the first laboratories of industrial research created by great American and European firms since the 1930s, replicating the organizational model of universities.

This structure is very common, because of the advantages it offers. It:

- promotes an effective organization of the main technical and scientific competencies needed for the innovation process;
- facilitates communication and interaction between specialists with the same background and scientific interest;
- favours in-depth research and the study of relevant problems in the medium/long term, creating an environment that motivates researchers.

Functional structures also enjoy high levels of efficiency, because of the ease of communication between specialists in the same field and the creation of a 'critical mass', necessary for having modern knowledge in every scientific field.

Functional structures also have drawbacks; problems arise especially when the R&D activity requires competencies from different fields of research. Under these conditions, severe problems of inter-departmental communication may arise, and the specialist contribution of each department may end up being handled in a non-integrated way without the necessary attention for the needs of users.

Another disadvantage of the functional structure is the impossibility to quickly adapt to changes in the research objectives, especially when these require rebalancing the weight of each field of research or the closing of one.

This structure, in fact, creates stable working groups inside departments that, over time, develop common cultures and languages, becoming very integrated and efficient; but at the same time they show great difficulty in cooperating with working groups from other disciplines and in receiving external news and stimuli.

To conclude, a functional structure is considered suitable for projects that involve a reduced number of scientific disciplines, in order to make departmental and project objectives coincident. It is an organizational structure which is mainly suitable for firms with low product diversification.

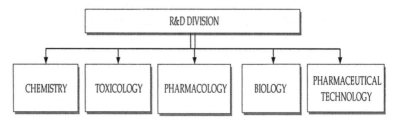

Figure 7.2   Functional structure, arranged for scientific fields, of a pharmaceutical firm

Product Lines Structure

The structure designed around product lines is characterized by a division of R&D activities so that each line of product innovations may be taken care of by a specific research unit (Figure 7.3).

In this structure, each innovation project is followed by one group of researchers performing all the work from the definition of the initial project to the conclusion and the consequent production; each research project is considered a specialized line of production and has a certain budget of resources. This solution does not eliminate the need for specialist knowledge in the various fields of research, but this knowledge is organized within each product research unit. This organizational structure allows the disadvantages of a functional structure to be avoided, especially in a firm which is highly diversified in product innovation lines and processes. In such cases the amount of resources and knowledge required for R&D is very diversified, because of the specialization and the fragmentation of knowledge, due to scientific and technical progress. Under such conditions a functional structure is not capable of elaborating the amount of information the firm receives, making forecasts and suitable evaluations, or deciding the tasks each new product line has to carry out.

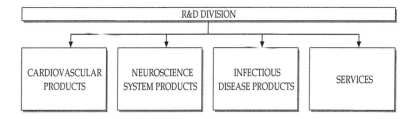

*Figure 7.3   Product lines structure, arranged for therapeutic areas, of a
pharmaceutical firm*

The product line structure allows competences and resources to be assigned more efficiently, according to the specific needs of each product or process innovation line. This model also has a higher managerial and organizational flexibility, enabling an easier coordination of activities within each project and an easier focalization of the activities toward cost and time objectives.

Project Structure

This organizational structure is characterized by the way resources are assigned to the various research projects. This assignment is *temporary* and lasts until the completion of the project; once the project is finished the resources are absorbed back into the assets of the R&D department.

This organizational structure implies a specialization of the resources and the organization of working groups around the various projects; the project manager has authority over the working group of the specific project, whose size can vary from a few to hundreds of people.

The project structure is preferable when:

- it is necessary to reach a complex result in a definite time span and to exert greater control over the project;
- time is a crucial factor;
- the aggregation of resources and competences belonging to different units is required and the project is new for the research structure;
- there is a high interdependence, due to technical reasons.

The advantages mostly derive from the better control over the project, better relations with clients and a greater reliability of the result. The disadvantages derive from the difficulties in relations and in the scientific update of researchers with the same background, taking care of the various projects and working for different managers in different places, often quite distant from each other and from their functional department for long periods of time.

Moreover, such organization may determine conditions of over- or under-exploitation of specialist resources, because of the discontinuous nature of the innovation projects and the difficulty of quickly reallocating resources from project to project. For these reasons, project structures perform better in the advanced phases of the innovation cycle, when projects require a strong integration between the various disciplines, they have binding deadlines and their success is crucial for the firm.

Matrix Structure

The matrix structure is characterized by the presence of both function-specialized units and project-specialized units. The R&D system is divided into functional areas, specialized in various fields of science, and into different research projects, each with a temporarily assigned group of scientists.

In other words human resources are organized in functional departments according to their field of study and are temporarily assigned to a research project, so they can offer their specialist knowledge under the supervision of a product manager, but at the same time keep their position inside the functional department to which they belong (Table 7.6). This solution permits matching the advantages of the functional and project models.

In the matrix structure, functional managers have to recognize the authority of the project manager for decisions having an impact on project results, costs and time for realization. The project manager handles the research group, addresses and coordinates the assigned resources and is in charge of the advancement and the final results of the project. The functional directors, on the other hand, are responsible for planning, managing and developing their pool of specialists and the methodologies used. In the matrix structure the project and functional managers are, therefore, jointly in charge of the objectives of each research project.

The double authority system, typical of the matrix structure, does not only have drawbacks. It is true that it can determine ambiguities, conflicts and stress, but it can also improve the chances of professional growth, creating more managerial positions and at the same time improving communication and decisional autonomy. This structure also allows the development of highly specialized resources and the coordination of the resources needed by innovative projects requiring rapid adjustments to environmental changes and quick elaboration of information.

Such a structure can be adopted with good results, if the three following conditions occur:

- the existence of R&D activities contemporarily demanding specialist knowledge and unitary vision of the innovation process;
- R&D activities requiring a system with a great capacity for elaborating information;
- the possibility of employing human resources with flexibility, so that each specialist can work at the same time in different tasks, being ready to move to another task.

Table 7.6   Matrix structure

	Department Field A	Department Field B	Department Field C	Department Field D
Project 1	A1	B1	C1	D1
Project 2	A2	B2	C2	D2
Project 3	A3	B3	C3	D3
Project 4	A4	B4	C4	D4

The difficulty of handling R&D with a double command system produces in practice different shapes of the matrix structure, according to the division of power between department and project managers.

The *weak matrix* or functional matrix is characterized by project managers not having the hierarchical power over the human and technical resources working on the project; such authority remains within the power of the functional director. As a consequence of such a power imbalance, conflicts often arise in organizations between functional and project managers.

A substantial rebalancing of powers can be found in the *balanced matrix*, where the functional manager and the project manager substantially have the appropriate powers. This equilibrium does not necessarily have to be perfect; it depends on the firm's characteristics.

In the so-called *strong matrix*, or project matrix, the balance of power is in the favour of project managers: the departments supply human and technological resources to the project manager, only maintaining a role of scientific and technical support.

THE CHOICE OF THE ORGANIZATIONAL MODEL OF R&D ACTIVITIES

The relevant factors to be considered for the choice of the organizational structure for managing R&D activities are the following (Grandi and Tagliavento 2004).

Technological evolution. If new technologies develop very quickly, such as in the biotech and material science sectors, it is crucial for the firm to have a presence in the research fields which are more relevant for the innovation process. In this case, the functional structure appears to be the more suitable for maintaining the presence in the various research fields.

Number of research projects and relative diversity among them. The high number of research projects to be carried out and differences among them makes the job of the functional managers really complex, therefore a project structure for R&D activities is preferred.

Interdependence among different phases of the project development. When the project is characterized by high interdependence among the different phases of the innovation process and the fields of research involved, a matrix structure for R&D is preferable. It assures more efficient coordination mechanisms, quicker information exchange and a better capability in handling research phases requiring different research fields.

Costs. If scientific and technological activities are characterized by relevant scale economies, the project organization may not be appropriate, because of its high costs and the difficulty in assigning the resources needed for their indivisibility. This happens especially when a research laboratory requires instruments operating at low unit costs only on a large volume of activity or when a minimum number of researchers is necessary for obtaining a balanced mix of resources or the availability of rare and qualified competences. In such cases a functional R&D organization works better, both in terms of efficiency and effectiveness.

THE INNOVATION SYSTEM AND THE OPERATIONAL SYSTEM

However, it should be noted that the firm innovation system, even if highly autonomous, will have to keep close relationships with the other firm sub-systems, in particular marketing and production, in order to offer its contribution to the firm's growth.

The marketing system must have the capacity for understanding the arising needs of the market, in order to provide useful information for the design of new products and for testing their acceptability. The production system must have an active role in supplying advice to the innovation system, using the experience gained so far.

The relevance of relationships between the innovation system of the firm and the external system represented by the scientific and technological world (universities, laboratories, etc.), for exchanging information and knowledge, should also be noted (Nelson 1993).

KEY ROLES IN MANAGING INNOVATION PROJECTS

The innovation is the result of the work of many people, interacting in various roles. Workers with technical and scientific competences are needed, but also people who believe in the project, who have communication and leadership skills and are able to assess the risks and gains of every project.

The experience of the most innovative firms also highlights the crucial role, in the most innovative results and products, of workers not formally recognized by the organizational structure. In these firms a structure of informal roles has been found, where people carry out the project along with the functional manager and/or the product manager. For successful projects, some key roles must be performed, formally or informally (Sobrero 1999). They are the following.

Ideas generator. First of all, every innovation needs an 'ideas generator', a person who has the ability to recombine information, technologies, processes and products already available on the market, imagining new products and services in an innovative way. The 'ideas generators' are usually technicians and specialists, capable of going over and above the technologies and the products currently available on the market. If this role is not adequately performed, the chances of generating innovation and progress are limited.

Internal entrepreneur. The role of this 'internal entrepreneur' is to recognize, put forward and demonstrate the advantages of a new technical idea or approach or procedure, in order to obtain the formal approval of management. He has to formulate an articulated and convincing project, capable of arousing interest, and gather the resources necessary for its realization. It is important that the internal entrepreneur has the capacity to single out the potential risks and gains of the project, pointing out its strengths and weaknesses.

Project leader. The project leader has the key role of guiding the project, coordinating and planning activities and resources with the purpose of putting an approved idea into practice. This role is crucial and very delicate for any project.

Gatekeeper. This key worker has the role of gathering and forwarding information from the internal and external environments. More precisely this activity consists in keeping track of the innovation and research carried out outside the firm, in order to: a) establish a connection between the research group knowledge and the external sources of information; b) spread the knowledge within the research group, using the knowledge acquired externally as a starting point. The absence of connections with the external environment and the other research groups inside the firm can be extremely harmful, because the researchers cannot compare their progress and the innovative potential of the project. Gatekeepers can also have an active role in training, developing and facilitating socialization within working groups. In performing these tasks they not only gather, translate and codify external information, but enable the researchers to have contacts with their colleagues operating outside the firm.

Sponsor of the project group. A project has to be supported and stimulated from outside. Informal support from some important managers can be crucial for protecting the project and avoiding members of the project being distracted from their research. The group sponsors are usually intermediate level managers operating at any level in the innovation system and recognizing the commercial relevance of the project.

In short, the effective running of the innovation system depends on the architecture of the system, the way it operates and the organization which performs the needed transformations. To maintain the firm's competitiveness over time and to continue creating value in a hypercompetitive environment it is necessary to think about the future, while exploiting the existing firm structure, so as to plan the change in the firm's structure and finally to manage the R&D activities so that they can create innovations in products and processes.

STRATEGY FOCUS: R&D SYSTEM MODELS IN SOME RELEVANT INDUSTRIES

The R&D System in Novartis

In Novartis the research is conducted primarily through the Novartis Institutes for Biomedical Research (NIBR), with headquarters in Cambridge, US and with locations worldwide. The centre is committed to innovation in drug discovery and the successful collaboration with academic institutions and biotechnology companies. The Cambridge facility is home to more than 1,300 scientists and technology experts.

Another important facility is in Basel, Switzerland, in close proximity to multiple renowned academic institutions and biotechnical companies with 1,500 scientists and technology experts.

Other NIBR facilities are in East Hanover and Emeryville in the US, Vienna, Austria and Tsukuba, Japan with 800 scientists and technology experts.

Corporate research at Novartis also comprises three independent institutes with a total staff of more than 750 scientists: The Genomics Institute of the Novartis Research Foundation (GNF), in La Jolla, California, The Novartis Institute for Tropical Diseases (NITD) in Singapore and The Friedrich Miescher Institute (FMI) in Basel, with a total of 750 researchers.

At the NIBR the resources and scientific expertise are organized into ten strategic disease areas:

- Autoimmunity & transplantation,
- Cardiovascular,
- Diabetes & Metabolism,
- Gastrointestinal,
- Infectious Diseases,
- Musculoskeletal Diseases,
- Neuroscience,
- Oncology,
- Ophthalmology,
- Respiratory Diseases.

Partnerships have been activated with academic, biotechnological and pharmaceutical companies.

Novartis has also formed strategic alliances and collaborations with other partners in the industry and with academic institutions, in order to develop new products, acquire platform technologies and to access new markets.

Up to one-third of annual Pharmaceutical Division R&D expenditures reach licensing agreements with other companies, particularly specialized biotechnology companies, so as to co-develop promising pharmaceutical compounds. These co-development and alliance agreements are intended to allow the Group to capitalize on the potential of these compounds and to expand its development pipeline. In 2005 and 2006, Novartis entered into more than 100 alliances, to complement internal R&D activities. In 2006 the company had 30 major development alliances with important companies within the pharmaceutical industry, such as Genentech, Idenix, Human Genome Sciences, 3M, Noven, Procter & Gamble, Schering-Plough, Sigma-Tau, Synosis, Orion, Mitsubushi, NexMed, etc.

From time to time, Novartis has also made equity investments in licensing partners or fully acquired companies to gain access to novel compounds, such as in the case of the acquisition of NeuTec Pharma in 2006.

The R&D System in the Marazzi Group

In the Marazzi Group more than 60 highly qualified people work in R&D activities, regarding the ceramic tile sector. A team dedicated to R&D operates within each Business Unit (Italy, Spain, Russia, France, USA).

The activity is autonomous in Italy (where approximately 50% of R&D resources operate), Russia and Spain, while in France the R&D activity is developed with the support of the Italian Ceramic Laboratory.

In particular the R&D system is organized in the following way:

- a laboratory for chemical and mineralogical activities, which studies chemical and physical characteristics of raw materials;
- a laboratory for testing materials and finished products;
- a laboratory for new products.

In Italy there is also a team dedicated to technological innovation in process and machinery. The R&D activity, through the research on materials and mixtures, contributes to the reduction of production costs and to the creation of new products.

The R&D Direction also participates in the process development projects together with the most important producers of technological innovation (Sacmi, System Tecnitalia, Nuova Firma and SIL). In addition the Group collaborates with universities and research institutes on the development of new processes and new technologies.

In 2006 the R&D expenses reached €5.3 million. Most of all the internal R&D activity on production process generates not patented know-how, such as formulas for slurry and solutions for tuning up processes.

The R&D System in the Fiat Group

Fiat is one of the major car makers in the world. It was founded in 1899 in Turin and since its origin development has followed two directions: internationalization and innovation. Over one century of activity, Fiat has been producing not only cars, but also airplanes, trains, commercial vehicles, buses, trucks, agricultural tractors and marine engines.

Fiat is today one of the principal European industrial groups, operating in 61 countries through 637 companies with 180 facilities (128 outside Italy); in 2006 it recorded €51.8 billion revenues (up 11.4% from 2005), with 172,012 employees, 96,000 of which were outside Italy. The Group is organized in ten sectors of activities (Table 7.7).

Product and process innovation plays an important part in Fiat Group strategies. In 2006 some 13,200 people were working in 116 Italian and foreign research centres, with annual expenses in R&D of €1.6 million or around 3.2% of net revenues of industrial activities (Table 7.8).

Table 7.7   Operating sectors and companies of the Fiat Group

Operating sectors	Companies	Net revenues (€ billion)
Automobiles	Fiat Auto	23.7
Ferrari & Maserati	Ferrari & Maserati	1.9
Agricultural & Construction Equipment	CNH	10.5
Trucks & Commercial Vehicles	Iveco	9.1
Fiat Powertrain Tech. (1)	FPT	6.1
Metallurgical Products	Teksid	0.9
Components	Magneti Marelli	4.4
Production Systems	Comau	1.3
Publishing & Communication	Isedi	0.4
Services	Business Solutions	0.7
Holding companies, other companies and eliminations		−7.4

Note: (1) FPT is the new sector which groups all car engine and transmission activities. Fiat regained control over these activities in May 2005 following termination of the Master Agreement with General Motors. Started in 2006, the sector also include the engine and transmission operations of Iveco, Centro Ricerche Fiat and Elasis.

Source: Fiat Annual Report 2006 and www. fiatgroup.com.

Each sector of activities has an internal structure dedicated to R&D for new products. All R&D activities are integrated by research with high innovative and cross content, developed by the Centro Ricerche Fiat and Elasis, the two scientific poles of the Group. The strategies of the two centres are coordinated by the Technical Committee of the Group Executive Council.

Thanks to its intense activity, Fiat has obtained relevant results in environment-compatible technological innovations of product and process.

Set up in 1976, the Centro Ricerche Fiat provides the Group with effective, innovative solutions at competitive prices, ensuring smooth technology transfer by further increasing the professional qualification of personnel through training.[14] This enables the Centre to play an active role in supporting technological growth for the Fiat Group, its partners and the communities where they work in fields such as motor vehicles and components, energy, safe and environmentally-friendly mobility, telematics, innovative materials and relevant technologies, mechatronics and optics.

In particular, the Centre's work in innovative power plant, alternative propulsion systems and transmissions is conducted through Powertrain Research and Technology headed by Fiat Powertrain Technologies, the Fiat Group sector set up in May 2005 which groups together all of the Group's activities in this area.

Table 7.8   Fiat facilities and research centres

Area	Plant	R&D centres
Italy	52	50
Europe (except Italy)	56	32
North America	25	15
Mercosur	20	10
Other areas	27	9
Total	180	116

Source: Fiat 2004 Annual Report.

In addition to its headquarters in Orbassano, on the outskirts of Turin, the Centro Ricerche Fiat has four branches in Bari, Catania, Trento and Foggia, as well as a controlling interest in the C.R.P. Plastics and Optics Research Centre in Udine, where work focuses on advanced research in the field of optics and plastics for automotive lighting systems.

With a staff of 870 employees, the Centro Ricerche Fiat made significant progress during the year, as witnessed by the 61 new patent applications it filed in 2006, bringing the total number of patents held by the Centre to over 2,100. A further 900 patents are currently pending. In addition, the Centro

Ricerche Fiat was awarded 128 projects in the EU's Sixth Framework Program, confirming its leadership in European research.

The Centro Ricerche Fiat cooperates with over 150 universities and research centres, and more than 750 industrial partners around the world. This network further strengthens the Centre's global innovation strategies, ensures that it can implement specific operations at the local level and helps it create skills and monitor its competitiveness and growth.

Set up in 1988 by the Fiat Group as a company dedicated to research work in the framework of development programmes for Southern Italy, Elasis has grown into a highly specialized research centre, whose work addresses technological innovation, complete vehicle development, mobility and its environmental impact, and traffic safety.[15] The Centre has two sites in Pomigliano and Lecce, both located in Southern Italy, with 765 employees and is provided with sophisticated computer-aided design and calculation tools and advanced physical and virtual testing equipment which are based on an ability to develop and manage information systems that puts Elasis in the front ranks of the world's R&D centres. At Elasis, work on engines and transmissions is carried out as part of Fiat Powertrain Technologies' development projects.

In 2006, Elasis continued to pursue its strategic objectives for forging new links in the research/innovation system's value chain and for promoting local development. In pursuing this objective, Elasis worked within consortia including universities and private institutions in basic research and training, continuing to sharpen its focus on the issues related to mobility and its environmental impact.

NOTES

1. On the importance, in general, of innovation management as a factor in the creation of a sustainable competitive advantage, see Hamel (2006).
2. Regarding the innovation process of a new drug, we can identify two macro-stages: research (or drug discovery) and new product development (development). Drug discovery includes basic research, screening activities and synthesis of the new chemical entity. Development is, on the other hand, the transformation activity of a new compound (NCE) into a drug and includes the pre-clinical and clinical tests of its effectiveness. The development activity is the longest and most expensive stage of the process. For more detailed studies, see: Pammolli (1996).
3. Porter (1985) talks precisely about 'activities of technological development' such as supporting activities to the strictly operating activities. On the importance of an organizational architecture directed at configuring a continuously innovating firm, see among others: Hargadon and Sutton (2000); Brown (2002); Levitt (2002).

4. The degree of integration of R&D activities can be measured by the ratio of costs of purchased R&D services and the total costs of R&D activities sustained by the firm in the considered period. The greater the ratio, the lower the integration degree will be.
5. On the advantages of externalization of research, see among others: Senn and Rubenstein (1989); Pisano (1990); Piccaluga (1996).
6. According to various authors, there is a structural weakness in small and medium enterprises (SME) in relation to the phenomenon of technological innovation, due basically to the limitations related to the development of the technological endowment of the firm as a whole regarding technological knowledge and organizational competences. On the importance of developing the technological endowment of SME through external growth processes, which favour focusing on a few technological competences and the adoption of external coordination methods, and on the related difficulties, see among others Boccardelli (2002).
7. Pisano (1990) analyses the option between make or buy in terms of *transaction costs* through an application to the biotech sector. In this industry it is practically impossible to evaluate the costs and the result of a specific research process in its initial phase; since the uncertainties which characterize R&D in general can only be faced as long as the project proceeds; the parts of a research contract usually agree upon the renegotiation of the contract as long as the uncertainties are solved and new products emerge. From this point of view, the behaviour of parties (commissioner and contractor/researcher) is influenced by the number and characteristics of other actors to whom the commissioner can possibly relate for the project transfer.
8. Protection of property rights is limited when: a) rights are not yet defined and only secrecy provides protection; b) even though property rights exist, the rapidity of change is high, while no technological standard is yet consolidated.
9. An empirical analysis of transformation in the organization of innovation activities in the pharmaceutical field, following the evolution of scientific and technological knowledge bases, has been conducted by Pammolli (1996). Through the numeric representation of agreement networks and licence contracts stipulated on a global scale between the second half of the 1970s and 1993, the author has analysed the evolution of the relational scope characterizing the innovation activities in the pharmaceutical sector following the introduction of biotechnologies.
10. As for example in the pharmaceutical industry with the advent of biotechnologies to the detriment of competences of synthesis chemistry.
11. On this issue see: Huston and Sakkab (2006).
12. On this subject see: Pisano, Shan and Teece (1988); Albertini and Butler (1995); Jones (2000); Gassmann, Reepmeyer and Zedtwitz (2004); Gassmann and Reepmeyer (2005).
13. There are some cases, like in the biotechnological sector, in which quick technological change makes existing competencies obsolete, as well as firms already operating in the market. Also see Tushman and Anderson (1986).
14. Source: 2005 and 2006 Fiat annual reports.
15. Source: 2006 Fiat annual report. Further information is available on the Centre's website at www.elasis.it.

8. The sustainability of value in highly competitive industries

INTRODUCTION AND OBJECTIVES

This chapter summarizes the determinants of firm value in highly dynamic industries. For the sustainability of value it is necessary to systematically create innovations of product and process, reconfiguring the firm structure.

The models developed in the previous chapters allow the relevant variables for the value to be identified and the fundamental relationships among them to be pointed out. Through simulations it is possible to define the conditions for an innovation strategy that can create value. In this way top management can evaluate the return and the risk of the strategy and decide whether to invest in the firm or not.

In order to create value, top management is required to have a clear vision of the business evolution and an ability for developing and organizing R&D resources and competences, in accordance with a consistent design.

Product and process innovations, organizational development and R&D resources are, therefore, at the core of the sustainability of value, especially in the most dynamic sectors.

DEFENDING THE COMPETITIVE ADVANTAGE FROM IMITATION AND MOBILITY OF STRATEGIC RESOURCES

Once a new competitive advantage over competitors, through new products or production processes, has been acquired, the interest of a firm is to exploit the superior performance and protect it as long as possible until a new product or process is launched on the market. To this aim, it can be useful to erect temporary barriers, so that new products and processes cannot be easily imitated, resulting in a longer lasting competitive advantage.

Since a relevant and important barrier to imitation of the new products or processes comes directly from property rights, the innovator will use patents and registered trademarks, for obtaining legal protection, based on the heavy sanctions relating to the violation of these rights.

Effective barriers to imitation also come from the firm's and product's brand and its reputation. These intangible assets are difficult to imitate, because they are the result of a company's activity over time, that is the accumulation of knowledge, and thus they share a very close connection with the specific structure of the firm (path dependency).

Other effective barriers to imitation are the following.

Scale economies in production: a highly efficient scale of production can represent an obstacle to entry in the market for a potential competitor, because its entry will produce a large increase of supply with a consequent reduction in product prices and post-entry profits.

Existence of complementary resources: when the firm's competitive advantage originates from the interrelation between its different resources, product imitation is more difficult, because it does not replicate the conditions for the advantage.

Causal ambiguity: often, the most relevant obstacle to imitation is constituted by the difficulty in decoding which factors enable the competitive advantage; in these cases the innovating firm will have to actively hide this information from the market.

Deterrence: the threat of retaliation by the enterprise to harm the imitator can also be used to defend the competitive advantage.

Since a serious threat to the sustainability of a firm's competitive advantage originates from the mobility of strategic resources to competitors, the innovating firm will have to prevent this, by creating effective obstacles to the resources' mobility.

Strategic resources are, for example, the specialized skills and knowledge in R&D, the communication and interactive abilities, specific technological capabilities, the technical and scientific employees, the technological know-how, etc. To this aim the firm will favour the diffusion of tacit knowledge, avoiding operation manuals, etc. since codified resources are easily transferable. Tacit knowledge can be transferred as well, because it moves with the person that holds it, but it is characterized by a strong causal ambiguity that makes its evaluation from outside the firm really complex. For this reason, the acquisition of such knowledge is a risky activity.

As an authoritative literature pointed out, a firm will benefit from a more durable competitive advantage when its strategic resources and competences are complex and firm specific (Schendel and Hofer 1979; Hamel and Heene 1994; Prahalad and Hamel 1990; Barney 1991; Grant 1991; Peterlaf 1993; Collis and Montgomery 1997).[1]

Resources complexity occurs when strategic resources are strongly interdependent with the others and it is difficult to evaluate their effectiveness. Are the marketing director and his staff those making the firm successful or is it the system in which they work? In many cases it is difficult to understand where the competitive advantage originates, because resources and results cannot be evaluated separately.

Resources specificity is when they are tightly linked to the organization of the firm, so these resources are much less mobile and cannot be successfully used by other firms. As an example, consider a very skilled manager whose experience is very specific to a certain small sector of operations.

Since the sustainability of value is threatened by imitation and substitution, the top management has to carefully consider these threats by making effective barriers to imitation and mobility of strategic resources. However, this approach is not sufficient; the continuous investment in resources and capabilities is the key to maintaining the competitive advantage over the long haul (Grant 1998; Porter 1991).

CREATING NEW COMPETITIVE ADVANTAGES AND VALUE THROUGH INNOVATION STRATEGIES

As we saw in the previous chapters, defending the competitive advantage is useful in the short term, but it is not effective in the long term, especially in highly innovative and dynamic sectors, where competition is strong and the evolution of demand unpredictable. In these environments, even well structured organizations, endowed with superior resources and skills, can be quickly pushed out of the market, with the barriers created to protect them rapidly broken.

The thesis we affirm is that the competitive advantage obtained by the firm is temporarily effective; it cannot be defended by barriers in the long run, but it can be re-established only by innovations in processes and products.[2]

Consider the crises that affected well established firms, such as Ford and General Motors, endowed with relevant resources and competences. The same process explains cases of success based on innovation as well. In the 1970s Honda was smaller than American Motors and had not started to export to the USA; Toyota was tiny compared to any great American firm in the automotive sector; Canon was not comparable to the superpower of Xerox; and Komatsu's sales were around 35% of those of its competitor Caterpillar.

Therefore, in sectors characterized by high dynamic and competitiveness the only way to maintain a competitive edge and continue creating value in the long run is by innovating processes and products, according to the environmental trends changing the market.

A successful strategy does not live in the past but for the future, based on a clear view of structural changes in the economic environment. It must define how to restructure the firm's organization in relation to the innovation to be introduced. Only by recognizing the new opportunities and creating new technological and organizational processes will it be possible to sustain the firm's value in such competitive sectors.

With reference to the most important environmental trends, we have identified three models of industries and three alternative innovation strategies:

- process innovation strategy;
- product innovation strategy;
- integrated innovation strategy.

THE ECONOMIC CONDITIONS FOR PROCESS INNOVATION STRATEGIES THAT CREATE VALUE

Process innovation strategies are absolutely necessary in industries characterized by substantially homogeneous products, where fundamental trends are represented by process innovations, caused by technical progress embodied in new plant and production processes (type A industries). These innovations induce increases in productivity factors and consequent reductions in costs and prices.

In these industries firms mainly compete on costs. The strategy to be adopted consists in increasing the productivity levels of factors through innovations of plant and equipment (process innovation strategies).

Which are the economic conditions that are consistent with innovation strategies creating value? The analytical model developed in Chapter 4 points out the relevant variables and the fundamental relations to be satisfied, so that the strategy can create value. To be exact, the conditions for a strategy creating value are defined by the following relations:

$$Vs = \sum_{t=1}^{T} \{[C_L(0)a^t + M(0)b^t - C_L(0)(1 + r + s)^t] Q(t)(1 - \tau^*)\} / (1 + \rho)^t$$

$$- I(0) > 0 \qquad (8.1)$$

$$C_L(0)a^T + M(0)b^T - C_L(0)(1 + r + s)^T = 0 \qquad (8.2)$$

where:
$$a = \frac{1+s}{1+\lambda_L} \; ; \; b = \frac{1+s}{1+\lambda_I}$$

Among the well known symbols, Vs is the strategy value, τ^* is the adjusted tax rate, $Q(t)$ is the volume of sales; T is the economic duration of process life, ρ the cost of capital, λ_L the rate of increase of labour productivity, λ_I the rate of increase of labour productivity in a capital goods industry, s the inflation rate.[3]

In particular, expression (8.1) prescribes that the present value of free cash flows from operations, discounted at the cost of capital ρ, must be greater than the capital invested in the new production structure $I(0)$.[4]

Equation (8.2) prescribes that, in the hypothesis of a residual value of the production structure equal to zero, the lifetime T of the production structure cannot be longer than the period after which the unit cash flow becomes equal to zero from positive values.[5]

The above relations indicate that the value of a process innovation strategy depends on environment trends, expressed by the parameters s, ρ, λ_L, λ_I, and on the industry conditions influencing sale price dynamics and the structure of the firm j influencing its operating costs. The model also emphasizes the importance of the investment in new equipment $I(0)$ and the unit margin $M(0)$ on product cost.

From a theoretical point of view, the model clearly identifies the economic conditions for a strategy creating value, in a dynamic context regarding the industry and the firm competitive positioning. From a practical point of view, the model allows the top management to choose the strategy, verifying the risk and the return of alternative innovation strategies. First, it is a matter of simulating the results of different price policies and investments under different environmental trends, then of verifying the consistency of the required margin and the investment with the industry structure and expected technical progress. Similar valuations will regard the other relevant variables having an influence on the firm value.

If the company results as not being capable of creating value, a quick exit from the industry must be planned, to avoid an irreversible process of value disruption. Generally, the higher the rate of technical progress and productivity increase (λ_L), the harder it will be for the firm to continue the game, especially if its competitive position is weak, compared to its competitors. In addition, creating value will be more difficult when innovation is endogenous and it has to be produced within the same company that will use it. This will require organizing an effective R&D structure within the firm. Finally, an increasingly competitive environment, reducing product prices, can make it impossible for the less efficient firms to continue creating value.

In order to point out how the model can be used, let us consider a firm operating in a type A industry, with the following data (Table 8.1).

Table 8.1   Process innovation strategies creating value: simulation data

Environmental trends		
Rate of increment of labour productivity (λ_L)	0.04	0.07
Rate of increment of labour productivity in equipment industry (λ_I)	0.04	0.07
Rate of increment of maintenance costs (r)	0.05	
Cost of capital (ρ)	0.10	
Rate of inflation (s)	0.03	
Adjusted tax rate (τ^*)	0.25	

Firm variables		
Investment $I(0)$ (€)	100,000,000	
Capital intensity	10	
Labour cost per unit product $C_L(0)$ (€)	8.0	
Other product cost per unit (€)	7.0	
Quantities (Q) sold yearly	10,000,000	8,000,000
Unit product cost (€), $Cu(0)$	15.0	$M(0)/Cu$ %
Unit margin $M(0)$ (€)	4.0	26.6
	5.0	33.3
	6.0	40.0
	7.0	46.6
	8.0	53.3

Applying the analytical model, it is possible to calculate the economic conditions for innovation strategies that can create value, that is the set of firm decision variables and environment trends producing a positive value of the innovation strategy.

The function Vs (M, λ_L) is pictured in Figure 8.1. It indicates the relation between the unit margin $M(0)$ and the value of the innovation strategy, under the hypotheses of a rate of increase in labour productivity $\lambda_L = 0.04$ and 0.07. In the first case the unit margin has to be larger than 6 (40% on the unit cost); in the second case, the unit margin has to be larger than 7 (47% on the unit margin). As you can see, the higher the rate of labour productivity, the higher will be the required margin $M(0)$ for the innovation strategy that can create value.

Also the period of positive $EBITDA(T)$ varies according to the unit margin $M(0)$; for example it is equal to eight years with $M(0) = 8$ (53% on product cost) and equal to four years with $M(0) = 4$ (26.6% on product cost).

The rate of increase of productivity λ_L also reduces the period of positive $EBITDA(T)$, *ceteris paribus*; this is equal to six years with $M(0) = 8$ and equal to three years with $M(0) = 3$.

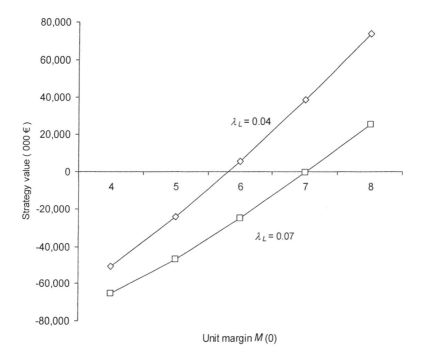

Figure 8.1   Process innovation strategies creating value ($Q(0) = 10,000,000$)

The volume of production and sales $Q(0)$ obtained by the investment also has a strong influence on the strategy value, as you can see comparing the function *Vs* in Figure 8.1 ($Q(0)$ = 10,000,000) and in Figure 8.2 ($Q(0)$ = 8,000,000), all other variables remaining unchanged. In the case λ_L = 0.04, the required unit margin $M(0)$ will be larger than seven, while it will be larger than eight in the case λ_L = 0.07.

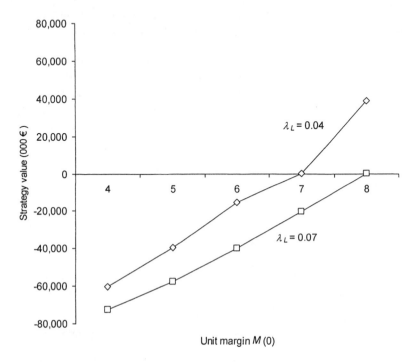

Figure 8.2   Process innovation strategies creating value ($Q(0)$ = 8,000,000)

These simulations also allow the top management to evaluate the effects of lower volumes of sales with respect to planned sales, or of higher investments in the new plant and equipment $I(0)$ with respect to those programmed. This permits the evaluation of the risk of innovation strategies.

THE ECONOMIC CONDITIONS FOR PRODUCT INNOVATION STRATEGIES THAT CREATE VALUE

The second model is represented by industries characterized by product innovation, where the main environmental trends are both the change in consumers' tastes and behaviour and the innovation of products. In these industries the innovation of product types and models is the winning strategy. The strategy for creating value by product innovation also requires planning investment in R&D activities. The analytical model developed in Chapter 5 points out the relevant variables and the fundamental relations to be satisfied so that the strategy can create value.

Precisely, the economic conditions for a strategy creating value are defined by the following relations:

$$Vs = \sum_{t=1}^{T} [P(0)(1+s-\gamma)^t - C(0)(1+s)^t] Q(t)(1-\tau^*)/(1+\rho)^t$$

$$- [I(0) + I_{MK}(0) + I_{R\&D}(0)] > 0 \qquad (8.3)$$

$$P(0)(1+s-\gamma)^T - C(0)(1+s)^T = 0 \qquad (8.4)$$

where: in addition to the already known symbols, Vs is the value of the strategy; $I(0)$ is the investment in production capacity, $I_{R\&D}(0)$ the R&D investment (that is the flow of R&D expenses capitalized at $t = 0$) and $I_{MK}(0)$ the marketing investment for the launch of the new product; γ the rate of price reduction for the aging of the product due to the innovations in the industry, T the economic duration of product life.

In particular, equation (8.3) prescribes that the present value of cash flows from operations discounted at the cost of capital ρ must be greater than the total capital invested in the new product. Equation (8.4) prescribes that the lifetime T of the product can be longer than the period after which the unit cash flow becomes equal to zero from positive value.

From a theoretical point of view, the model highlights the fundamental variables that influence the value of a product innovation strategy: the prices and the sales quantities of the new product, the amount of the required investment, the cost of capital and the technical progress.

From a practical point of view, the proposed model allows the calculation of the value of alternative innovation strategies. Different hypotheses on prices and quantities sold allow the calculation, through a simulation process, of the value of strategies that are consistent with different market situations and different environmental trends.

In particular, for creating value, the innovation strategy will require prices and quantities generating cash flows adequate to the required investment, during the life of the new product, but price policies and quantities sold have to be consistent with the structural condition of industry, while the life T of a new product depends on the technical progress and the competitors' pressure in the industry.

Generally, the higher the rate of product innovation in the industry, the harder it will be to continue creating value, especially if the competitive position of the firm is weak compared to its competitiors.

In order to point out the way the model can be used, consider a firm operating in a type B industry, with the following data regarding the firm and the main enviromental trends (Table 8.2).

Table 8.2   Product innovation strategies creating value: simulation data

Environmental trends		
Rate of product price reduction (γ)	0.05	0.08
Cost of capital (ρ)	0.10	
Rate of inflation (s)	0.02	
Adjusted tax rate (τ^*)	0.25	
Firm variables		
Investment $I(0)$ (in €)	400,000,000	
Capital intensity $I(0)/Q(0)$	6,666	
Cost per unit product $C_U(0)$ (€)	14,000	
Quantities (Q) sold at $t = 0$	60,000	50,000
Rate of variation of quantities sold during the life cycle	$\varphi_1 = 0.10$ (years 1, 2) $\varphi_2 = 0.05$ (years 3, 4) $\varphi_3 = -0.10$ (years 5, 6) $\varphi_4 = -0.20$ (years > 6)	$P(0)/Cu$ in %
Product price $P(0)$ (€)	17,000	121
	18,000	128
	19,000	136
	20,000	143
	21,000	150
	22,000	157

The total investment in the new product is equal to €400,000,000 and the volume of sales at the launch stage equals 60,000 (or 50,000) units; in the following stages sales will increase at an annual rate of 0.10 for the first two years and 0.05 for the second two years; then sales will decrease at a rate of 0.10 for two years and 0.20 for the remaining product life. The unit cost of the new product is assumed to be equal to €14,000.

Under these conditions, the strategy value will depend on the price policy and the lifetime of the new product, which in turn depend on the environmental trends (technical progress, cost of capital, etc.) and the competitive pressure.

Applying the analytical model, it is possible to define, through simulation, the economic conditions, that is the set of firm decision variables and environmental trends, for innovation strategies creating value.

The function Vs (P, γ) is pictured in Figure 8.3. It indicates the relation between the product price policy $P(0)$ and the strategy value (Vs), under the hypotheses of a rate $\gamma = 0.05$ and 0.08, all other variables remaining constant.

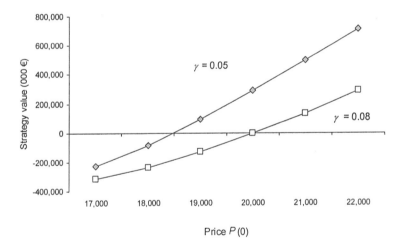

Figure 8.3   Product innovation strategies creating value with
            $Q(0) = 60,000$

The value of the strategy is very sensitive to the price level and the competitive pressure of the new products that influence the decrease rate of prices (γ) and the life duration of the new product (T) and therefore of positive cash flows. Also the volume of sales obtained by the new product $Q(0)$ has a strong influence on the innovation strategy value. This can be seen by comparing Figure 8.3 to Figure 8.4, which summarizes the result of a new simulation, considering $Q(0)$ = 50,000, all other variables remaining unchanged.

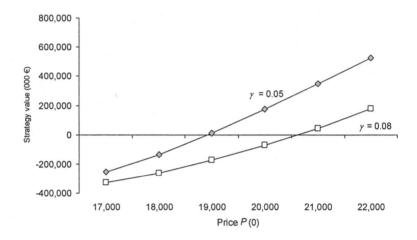

Figure 8.4   Product innovation strategies creating value with
              $Q(0) = 50,000$

This simulation will allow the top management to evaluate the risk of innovation strategies, on the basis of the expected environmental trends and competitive pressure.

THE ECONOMIC CONDITIONS FOR INTEGRATED INNOVATION STRATEGIES THAT CREATE VALUE

The third model (type C industries) is represented by industries where both process and product innovations are important. In these industries, in order to create value, the firm has to carry out an integrated strategy, pursuing productivity improvement and product innovation together.

According to the model developed in Chapter 6 the economic conditions for strategies creating value are defined by the following relations:

$$Vs = \sum_{t=1}^{T} \{[P(0)\,(1+s-\gamma-\delta)^t - C_j(0)(1+s)^t]\,Q(0)\,(1+\varphi)^t\,(1-\tau^*)/(1+\rho)^t\}$$

$$- [I(0) + I_{MK}(0) + I_{R\&D}(0)] \geq 0 \tag{8.5}$$

$$P(0) (1 + s - \gamma - \delta)^T - C_j(0) (1 + s)^T = 0 \tag{8.6}$$

where, in addition to the well-known symbols, $I(0)$ is the investment in the new plant, $I_{R\&D}(0)$ is the investment in R&D and $I_{MK}(0)$ the investment in marketing, T the economic duration of the investment, γ the rate of price decreasing as a consequence of competitors' new products and δ the rate of price decline as a consequence of the reducing cost of the new products caused by the new production processes with lower costs; φ the rate of variation of the new product sales after the launch stage.

The value of the strategy depends on the required investment, the tendencies of industry, expressed by the rates φ, γ, δ, s, and on the prices policy, according to the relations pointed out.

The model shows that, other variables being equal, the higher the price of the new product and the longer the life of the new product, the greater the value of the strategy.

Obviously, each price level $P(0)$ of the new product produces a different volume of sales $Q(0)$, in relation to the elasticity of the new product demand and consequently to the success of the product innovation. Therefore the limits of the prices policy are determined by market conditions and the success of the innovative processes.

The product life of the investment depends not only on the product innovation rate in the industry, which influences γ, but also on the innovation rate of productive processes, which affects δ. Thus, the deterioration process of prices and revenues is stressed by the cumulative effect due to product and process innovations.

The size of the required investment for implementing the strategy is also important. Incidentally, we observe that the investments for the new product also include the goodwill required to make the new product known and quickly reach the sales target.

In order to estimate the value of the strategy, it is possible to proceed by simulations. It is a matter of calculating an initial price $P(0)$, estimating the matching value of $Q^*(0)$ on the basis of market research, and calculating the strategy value, considering that a product's life depends on these quantities. By repeating these attempts it is possible to find, through a simulation process, the values of $P(0)$ and T, consistent with the market conditions satisfying the relations as above. If the strategy value is negative, because of the environment trends and the market conditions, it will be necessary to revise the investment plan and consider a new development strategy. If the expected income flow does not produce adequate yield on the invested capital, the best solution will be leaving the industry or liquidating the firm.

In order to point out the way the model can be used, let us consider a firm operating in a type C industry, with the following data regarding the firm and the environmental trends (Table 8.3).

Table 8.3   Integrated innovation strategies creating value: simulation data

Environmental trends		
Rate of price reduction for product innovations (γ)	0.05	0.10
Rate of price reduction for process innovations (δ)	0.03	
Cost of capital (ρ)	0.10	
Rate of inflation (s)	0.02	
Adjusted tax rate (τ^*)	0.25	

Firm variables		
Investment $I(0)$ (€)	400,000,000	
Capital intensity $I(0)/Q$	800	
Cost per unit product $C_U(0)$ (€)	400	
Quantities (Q) sold at $t = 0$	500,000	400,000
Rate of variation of quantities sold	$\varphi_1 =$ 0.08 (years 1, 2) $\varphi_2 =$ 0.04 (years 3, 4) $\varphi_3 = -0.10$ (years 5, 6) $\varphi_4 = -0.20$ (years > 6)	$P(0)/Cu$ in %
Product price $P(0)$ (€)	600	150
	700	175
	800	200
	900	225
	1,000	250
	1,100	275

In particular, the total investment in the new product and the new process is supposed as being egual to €400,000,000 and the volume of sales of the new product at the launch stage equal to 500,000 units.

Applying the analytic model, the value of alternative strategies can be calculated, varying the price policy $P(0)$ and assuming different environmental trends ($\gamma = 0.05$ or 0.10) and sales of the new product (500,000 or 400,000).

The results of these simulations are pointed out in Figure 8.5 and Figure 8.6, where the function $Vs(P, \gamma)$ is pictured, with respect to different values in $P(0)$ and $\gamma = 0.05$ and 0.10.

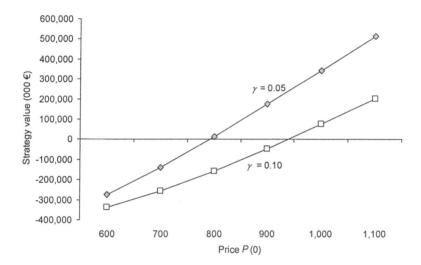

Figure 8.5 Integrated innovation strategies creating value with Q(0) = 500,000

The simulation clearly shows that it is not easy to create value, especially when the rate of technical advance, related to products and processes, is high. In fact, that means a quick deterioration of the competitive advantage and a short period (T) in which the firms may benefit from the advantage of product and process innovations. All that requires high margins and large volumes of sales.

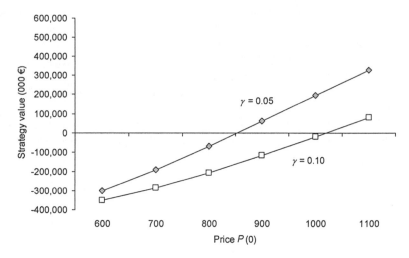

*Figure 8.6   Integrated innovation strategies creating value with Q(0) =
400,000*

THE SUSTAINABILTY OF FIRM VALUE IN HIGHLY COMPETITIVE INDUSTRIES

The previous analysis pointed out that the sustainability of firm value is a hard job in highly competitive environments. It has been demonstrated that firm value depends on unit margin, volume of sales, duration of investment life, investment and cost of capital, according to precise relations. Thus, only defined systems of these variables, with their patterns over time, are consistent with the creation of value.

In highly competitive environments, the sustainability of value is seen as being a very complex matter, because of the short duration of the economic life of investments, due to environmental trends, especially technical progress and changing customer behaviour. In these conditions, high unit margins and large sales volumes are required for creating value; the more important the investment in new processes and products, the greater they will be. But they can be obtained only if new products offer substantial differential benefits to customers, with respect to competitors' products, and the new production processes significantly reduce production costs. Therefore, product and process innovations are at the core of value creation in highly competitive environments.

DEVELOPING AND ORGANIZING R&D RESOURCES AND COMPETENCES TO CONTINUE CREATING VALUE

To ensure a flow of innovations necessary for the sustainability of value, firms have to accumulate resources and competences in R&D activities and organize them for carrying out the innovation process.

Focus on the innovation strategies allows identifying the resources and competences (or capabilities) the firm has to accumulate and protect from imitation and transfer to competitors, as well as those to develop or to acquire for carrying out the innovative process (Teece, Pisano and Shuen 1997).[6] For example, in the case of process innovations, resources and competences in the production system, technical know-how and engineering are strategic. In this way the innovation strategy becomes the means for guiding the change of the firm structure and particularly of the structure directed at creating continuous innovation by R&D activities.

It will be possible to define what resources and competencies must be acquired and built to carry out the innovative processes, what new channels should be explored right now and what new development priorities should be pursued right now to 'intercept the future' (Hamel and Prahalad 1994).

Thus it is very important to design the architecture of the R&D system properly – both the way it works and how effectively it motivates people in realizing the required transformations.

The alternative organizational structures of R&D and the criteria for designing the R&D structure suitable for developing innovation and creating new competitive edge have been examined in Chapter 7. The relevant factors to be considered for the choice of the organizational structure for managing R&D activities are the following: technological evolution, number of research projects and relative diversity among them, interdependence among different phases of the project development costs.

The analysis pointed out the strategic relevance of collaboration with other firms for extending knowledge, exploiting complementary resources and obtaining easier access to new knowledge and competences. Furthermore, thanks to collaboration, the firm has the possibility to share part of its R&D costs. This is particularly relevant in a highly competitive environment, where the change in technologies is very rapid and requires both large financial resources and high technical capabilities that a single firm does not always have.

Finally, the relevance of relationships between the firm and the external system represented by the scientific and technological world, universities, research laboratories and companies, for exchanging information and knowledge, has to be underlined.

TOP MANAGEMENT SKILLS AS A PRIMARY SOURCE OF COMPETITIVE ADVANTAGE AND VALUE

A reliable strategy requires an exact definition of objectives and the resources needed to obtain them in a systemic view of the company structure and of the environment. More precisely, an innovation strategy can be successful only if:

- it is coherent with the evolutionary trends of the environment and the future business evolution (business vision);[7]
- a reliable development plan for the firm structure, consistent with the resources and the competitive strength of the firm, is laid down;
- there are enough technological and organizational resources and competences to put the plan into effect.

All this indicates top management skills as primary sources of competitive advantage and firm value. To be precise, the capacity to create value principally depends on the top management capabilities of:

- viewing the future;[8]
- planning innovation and organizing the firm's innovation system;
- implementing the structural transformations of the firm;
- leading and motivating the workforce.

Future business vision means understanding the fundamental evolutionary trends that will affect competition in the sector. The analysis of future trends has to be based upon a deep understanding of macroeconomic, social and business trends shaping the sector: technological changes, shifts in the demographic and political situation, new lifestyles and so on (Drucker 1992; Becker and Freeman 2006).

It is important to understand, through experience and intuition, how these trends interact in affecting the industry.

To perceive the future of a sector, it is necessary to acquire in-depth knowledge in order to have an adequate understanding of potential discontinuities, of forces already at work in the market that potentially can change it radically (Hamel and Prahalad 1994 pp. 90–100). Future business vision also means a vision of changes in relevant resources and competences (Abell 1993) and, consequently, a vision of the changes for improvement of the firm structure.

Capabilities of planning innovation means the top management must be able to choose the innovation strategy and draw up a reliable development plan of the firm's structure, so as to reach objectives consistent with the environmental trends (Drucker 2002). This requires a deep knowledge of the old and the new processes for creating value.

Capabilities of organizing R&D means the top management is able to find effective organizational solutions to obtain superior performance (Dorgan, Dowdy and Rippin 2006) and systematically produce innovations. It means being able to create a firm innovation system, a working 'machine' suitable for realizing innovations.[9]

Capabilities of leadership means the top manager, the entrepreneur, has to have an authoritative leadership over the most qualified human resources, that is an ability to create a strategic intent (Hamel and Prahalad 1989), a shared system of values, building connections between people and guiding their operability coherently.[10]

All this means top managers must have rare, eclectic attitudes: a natural-born tendency to think differently, the capacity to have the future in mind instead of the present, an ability to organize, motivate and lead people and a natural empathy with human beings.

CONCLUSIONS

In highly dynamic and competitive industries, competitive advantage is temporary and a firm's value cannot be maintained or increased over time without product and process innovations and the consequent changes of firm structure. To create value the top management must look towards the future, identifying the fundamental environmental trends which are progressively eroding the competitive advantage of the firm and designing the change of the firm's structure, innovating the existing processes and products.

Identifying the strategy to pursue for rebuilding the competitive advantage and creating new value and evaluating the economic conditions under which an innovation strategy creates value is a very complex job. From a theoretical point of view it is a matter of strictly defining all relevant variables, the relations among them and their dynamics over time. From a practical point of view it is a question of offering a solution which is quite simple to use and at the same time capable of representing current situations.

For correctly defining the innovation strategy suitable for creating value, it is necessary, first of all, to identify the dominant trends of the industry, capable of modifying the conditions of competition. On these environmental trends a firm will have to base its innovation strategy, in order to create value.

The quantitative models described in Chapters 4, 5 and 6 provide an analytical approach to the complex problem of value creation in dynamic and competitive sectors. The proposed models allow a better understanding of how, and identify the internal and external conditions under which, the strategy creates value and the firm value can be maintained in the long run. That is to say they identify the links among the most relevant economic variables that need to be satisfied for creating value. Investments, prices, costs, the duration of the life of products and processes are closely linked by defined equations to technical progress, competitors' pressure and cost of capital, for a firm that can create value.

Through our models it is possible to simulate the set of values and thus of conditions coherent with the sustainability of firm value. Therefore, the proposed models can be used to verify whether the firm can survive or whether it is condemned, considering the competitive landscape changes.

The models can also be used to identify the resources and competences (or capabilities) the firm has to accumulate and protect from imitation and transfer to competitors, as well as those to be developed or acquired for carrying out the innovative process. In this way, the innovation strategy becomes the means for guiding the change of the firm structure and particularly the R&D structure directed at creating continuous innovations.

The proposed approach, linking firm strategy to finance and organization, aims at developing an effective structure for value-enhancing strategies, also promoting useful frames for guiding decisions. The choice of using an analytical approach, while it makes for a more rigorous analysis, certainly reduces the context in which it is applicable. Therefore, we hope that other scholars will examine different situations and propose more general models. In the same way, we hope that the relations between strategies and R&D structure will be further developed, also using experimental data.

NOTES

1. According to these authors only firm-specific and non-acquirable resources and skills can create the sustainability of competitive advantage in the long run. These resources and skills can be represented by certain production 'know-how', the access to crucial materials, the firm's reputation and image, brands and patents and so on. To be precise, according to the *resource-based theory*, the sustainability of competitive advantage relies upon the specificity and scarcity of resources and competences (capabilities) and the barriers to imitation and acquisition of them. Recent thinking in dynamic capabilities has extended the resource perspective, pointing out the importance of developing new resources and capabilities. See Teece, Pisano and Shuen (1997).
2. Sketching the outlines for building a dynamic theory of strategy, Porter (1991 and 1994, p. 449) aptly remarked: 'In a world where exogenous change is rapid or relatively continuous, however, the analytical problem becomes far more complicated. The value of past resources is continually depreciated or even rendered negative. The choice of strategy is a

series of ever changing games in which the position in one game can influence, but does not determine, the position in the next. Case after case illustrates that the leaders in one generation of products often fail to lead in the next ... A theory must give the firm latitude not only to choose among well defined options but to create new ones. The firm cannot be seen only optimizing within tight constraints, but should be represented as having the ability to shift the constraints through creative strategies choices, other innovative activity, and the assembly of skills and other needed capabilities.'

3. As seen in Chapter 1, τ^* is the fiscal rate on incomes revised in order to consider the fiscal benefits on depreciations.

4. The expression in brackets can be considered, with reasonable approximation, equivalent to the free cash flow from operations of the firm j. The difference is given by the variation of the net working capital; in the considered framework (absence of growth), we can assume this variation equal to zero.

5. This simplification can be accepted in practice, because much industrial equipment commonly has little, if any, salvage value. In addition, time discount makes this value, at the time of the investment decision, insignificant. However, in the cases where the ultimate scrap value of the equipment is expected to be significantly high, a simple approximation can be used. The approximation is to subtract the future estimated scrap value from its value when installed.

6. Teece, Pisano and Shuen (1997) call dynamic capabilities 'the capacity of integrating, creating and reconfiguring internal and external knowledge in order to face quick changes in the environment'. They extend the resource-based perspective, emphasizing the importance of developing new resources and competences suitable for creating new competitive edges that are difficult to imitate (dynamic capabilities approach). On the same issue see also Eisenhardt and Martin (2000); Teece and Pisano (1994).

7. On the environmental determinants of innovation see Porter (1994).

8. In a recent study Teece (2007) specifies and analyses the nature of dynamic capabilities. According to this author these capabilities are the foundation of sustainable enterprises' performance and they express the entrepreneurial function of top management.

9. The importance of good management practices to obtain superior performance is confirmed by the experiences of a number of firms and many empirical studies. Dorgan, Dowdy and Rippin (2006) recently completed a very interesting study on 700 manufacturing firms, showing that firms who usually use a number of well established management tools perform better on average than competitors that use these tools sporadically.

10. Hamel and Prahalad (1989) talk about *strategic intent* as a core factor for the success of many firms: 'Companies that have risen to global leadership over the past 20 years invariably began with ambitions that were out of all proportion to their resources and capabilities. But they created an obsession with winning at all organization levels and then sustained that obsession over the 10 to 20 year quest for global leadership. We term this obsession *"strategic intent"*...At the same time strategic intent is more than simply unfettered ambition (many companies possess an ambitious strategic intent yet fall short of their goals.) The concept also encompasses an active management process that includes focusing the organization's attention on the essence of winning, motivating people by communicating the value of the target, leaving room for individual and team contributions, sustaining enthusiasm by providing new operational definitions such as circumstances change, and using intent consistently in guiding resource allocations.' (Reprinted 2005, p. 150).

References

Abell D.F. (1993), *Managing with Dual Strategies. Mastering the Present, Preempting the Future*, New York: The Free Press.

Abernaty W.J. (1978), *The Productivity Dilemma*, New York: Johns Hopkins Press.

Adams W. and J. Dirlam (1966), 'Big Steel, Invention and Innovation', *Quarterly Journal of Economics*, 80 (2), 167–189.

Aizcorbe A., S.D. Oliner and D.E. Sichel (2006), 'Shifting Trends in Semiconductor Prices and the Pace of Technological Progress', Washington, Federal Reserve Board, working paper, 44.

Albertini S. and J. Butler (1995), 'R&D Networks in a Pharmaceutical Company: Some Implications for Human Resource Management', *R&D Management*, 25 (4), 377–393.

Amendola M. (1976), *Macchine, Produttività e Progresso tecnico*, Milano: Isedi.

Amendola M. and J.L. Gaffard (1988), *The Innovative Choice*, Oxford: Basil Blackwell.

Baba Y. (1989), 'The Dynamics of Continuous Innovation in Scale-Intensive Industries', *Strategic Management Journal*, 10, 89–100.

Bain J. (1956), *Barriers to New Competition*, Cambridge, MA: Harvard University Press.

Barney J.B. (1991), 'Firm Resources and Sustained Competitive Advantage', *Journal of Management*, 17, 99–120.

Barral P.E. (1997), *Twenty-two Years of Results in Pharmaceutical Research throughout the World (1975–1997)*, Puteaux Cedex: S.A. Edinter.

Bass F. (1969), 'A New Product Growth Model for Consumer Durables', *Management Science*, 16, January, 215–227.

Bass, F. (1980), 'The Relationship Between Diffusion Rate, Experience Curve and Demand Elasticities for Consumer Durable Technical Innovation', *Journal of Business*, 53, July, 51–67.

Becker W.M. and V.M Freeman (2006), 'Going from Global Trends to Corporate Strategy', *The McKinsey Quarterly*, 3, 17–26.

Berger S. (2005), *How to Compete*, New York: Currency Doubleday.

Besanko D., D. Dranove and M. Shanley (1996), *Economics of Strategy*, New York: Wiley.

Bierman H. and S. Smidt (1984), *The Capital Budgeting Decision*, New York: Macmillan.

Boccardelli P. (2002), *Innovazione Tecnologica e Strategia d'Impresa*, Milano: Franco Angeli.

Bonaccorsi, A. (2001), 'Innovazione Tecnologica e Strategie di Sviluppo delle Medie e Piccole Imprese', in F. Fontana and P. Boccardelli (eds), *L'innovazione Tecnologica nelle Medie e Piccole Imprese*, Roma: Luiss Edizioni.

Boston Consulting Group (1972), *Perspective on Experience*, BCG.

Brealey R.A. and S.C. Meyers (1996), *Principles of Corporate Finance*, New York: McGraw-Hill.

Brooke P.A. (1975), *Resistant Prices. A Study of Competitive Strains in the Antibiotics Markets*, Cambridge, MA: Bollinger.

Brown J. (2002), 'Research that Reinvents the Corporation', *Harvard Business Review*, August.

Bursi T. (1984), *Il settore meccano-ceramico nel comprensorio della ceramica: struttura e processi di crescita*, Milano: Franco Angeli.

Business Week (1999), 28 June.

Carroll G. and M. Hannan (2000), *The Demography of Corporation Industries*, Princeton: Princeton University Press.

Ceccanti G. (1996), *Corso di Tecnica imprenditoriale*, Padova: Cedam.

Chandler, A. (1969), *Strategy and Structure. Chapters in the History of the American Industrial Enterprise*, Cambridge, MA: The MIT Press.

Chandy R.K. and G.J. Tellis (1998), 'Organizing for Radical Product Innovation: the Overlooked Role of Willingness to Cannibalize', *Journal of Marketing Research*, 35.

Chesbrough H.W. and D. Teece (2002), 'Organizing for Innovation: When is Virtual Virtuous?', *Harvard Business Review*, August.

Clark K. (1987), 'Investment in New Technology and Competitive Advantage', in D.J.Teece, *The Competitive Challenge. Strategies for Industrial Innovation and Renewal*, Cambridge, MA: Ballinger.

Clark K.B. and T. Fujimoto (1991), *Product Development Performance: Strategy, Organization and Management in the World Auto Industry*, Boston, MA: Harvard Business School Press.

Cohen W.M. and D.A. Levinthal (1989), 'Innovation and Learning: the Two Faces of R&D', *Economic Journal*, 99, September.

Cohen W.M. and D.A. Levinthal (1990), 'Absorptive Capacity: a New Prospective on Learning and Innovation', *Administrative Science Quarterly*, 35.

Collis D.J. and C.A. Montgomery (1997), *Corporate Strategy. Resources and Scope of the Firm*, New York: McGraw-Hill.

Copeland T. and J.F. Weston (1988), *Financial Theory and Corporate Policy*, New York: Addison Wesley.

Copeland T., T. Koller and J. Murrin (1995), *Valuation. Measuring and Managing the Value of Companies*, New York: Wiley.

Daft R.L. (2001), *Organization Theory and Design*, South-Western College Publishing.

D'Aveni R. (1994), *Hypercompetition. Managing the Dynamics of Strategic Maneuvering*, New York: The Free Press.

Day G.S. (1999), *Market Driver Strategy. Processes for creating Value*, New York: The Free Press.

Day G.S. and D.J. Reibstein (1997), *Wharton and Dynamic Competitive Strategy*, New York: J.Wiley & Sons.

De La Mare R.F. (1977), 'Chemical Commodity Price Erosion', *Engineering and Process Economics*, 2.

Demura P. (1995), 'Productivity Change in the Australian Steel Industry. BHP Steel 1982–1995', Reserve Bank of Australia, *Productivity and Growth, Conference Volume*, edited by C. Kent, 173–184.

Dess G.G., A. Gupta, J.F. Hennart and C.W.L. Hill (1995), 'Conducting and Integrating Strategy Research at the International Corporate and Business Level: Issues and Directions', *Journal of Management*, 21, 357–393.

Di Masi J. (1991), 'Cost of Innovation in the Pharmaceutical Industry', *Journal of Health Economics*, 10 (2), 107–142.

Dorgan S.J., J.J. Dowdy and T.M. Rippin (2006), 'The Link between Management and Productivity', *The McKinsey Quarterly*, February, 1–7.

Dringoli A. (1980), *Margini sui Costi e Vita Economica degli Impianti. Politiche dei Prezzi e degli Investimenti*, Milano: Franco Angeli.

Dringoli A. (1989), 'Innovazioni Produttive, Attività di Sviluppo e Valutazione dei Progetti', *Finanza, Marketing e Produzione*, 2, June, 25–62.

Dringoli A. (1995), *Struttura e Sviluppo dell'Impresa Industriale*, Milano: McGraw-Hill.

Dringoli A. (2000), *Economia e Gestione delle Imprese. Modelli e Tecniche per la Gestione*, Padova: Cedam.

Dringoli A. (2006), *La Gestione dell'Impresa*, Padova: Cedam.

Dringoli A. (2007), *Strategie d'Innovazione e Valore*, Padova: Cedam.

Drucker P. (1985), 'The Discipline of Innovation', *Harvard Business Review*; Reprinted in *Harvard Business Review* (2002), August, 95–103.

Drucker P. (1992), *Managing for the Future: the 1990s and Beyond*, New York: Dutton.

Eisenhardt K.M. and J.A. Martin (2000), 'Dynamic Capabilities: What are They?', *Strategic Management Journal*, 21, 1105–1121.

Flamm K. (2003), 'Moore's Law and the Economics of Semiconductor Price Trends', *International Journal of Technology Policy and Management*, 3 (2), 127–141.

Freeman C. (1968), 'Chemical Process Plant: Innovation and the World Market', *National Institute Economic Review*, August, 45.

Freeman C. (1974), *The Economics of Industrial Innovation*, Baltimore: Penguin Books.

Gassmann O. and G. Reepmeyer (2005), 'Organizing Pharmaceutical Innovation: from Science-based Knowledge Creators to Drug-oriented Knowledge Brokers', *Creativity and Innovation Management*, 14 (3), 233–245.

Gassmann O., G. Reepmeyer and M. von Zedtwitz (2004), *Leading Pharmaceutical Innovation Trends and Drivers for Growth in the Pharmaceutical Industry*, Berlin: Springer.

Ghemawat P. (1985), 'Building Strategy on the Experience Curve', *Harvard Business Review*, March–April, 143–149.

Ghemawat P. (1991), *Commitment. The Dynamic of Strategy*, New York: The Free Press.

Gold B. (1976), 'Tracing Gaps between Expectations and Results of Technological Innovation: The Case of Iron and Steel', *The Journal of Industrial Economics*, 25 (1), Sept., 1–28.

Grabowski H. and J. Vernon (1990), 'A New Look at the Returns and Risks to Pharmaceutical R&D', *Management Science*, 36 (7), July, 804–821.

Grandi A. and M.R. Tagliavento (2004), 'Organizzare la Ricerca e lo Sviluppo di Nuovi Prodotti', in F. Munari and M. Sobrero (eds), *Innovazioni Tecnologiche e Gestione d'Impresa*, Bologna: Il Mulino.

Grant R.M. (1991), 'The Resource-Based Theory of Competitive Advantage. Implications for Strategy Formulation', *California Management Review*, Spring, 119–135.

Grant R.M. (1998), *Contemporary Strategy Analysis*, Malden, MA: Blackwell.

Guerci G.M. (2002), 'Lo Sviluppo Tecnologico dell'Industria Italiana', working paper, Milano, June.

Hamel G. (2006), 'Management Innovation', *Harvard Business Review*, February, 72–84.

Hamel G. and A. Heene (1994), *Competence Based Competition*, New York: Wiley.

Hamel G. and C.K. Prahalad (1989), 'Strategic Intent', *Harvard Business Review*, 67, (3), 63–76. Reprint in *HBR*, July–Aug. 2005, 148–161.

Hamel G. and C.K. Prahalad (1994), *Competing for the Future*, Boston: Harvard Business School Press.

Hargadon A. and R.I. Sutton (2000), 'Building Innovation Factory', *Harvard Business Review*, May–June, 157–166.

Harrigan K.R (1986), *Managing for Joint Venture Success*, Lexington: Lexington Books.

Hax A.C. and N.S. Majluf (1984), *Strategic Management*, Englewood Cliffs, NJ.: Prentice Hall.

Hayes R.H. and S.C. Weelwright (1984), *Restoring our Competitive Edge: Competition through Manufacturing*, New York: Wiley.

Herrmann A., T. Tomczak and R. Befurt (2006), 'Determinants of Radical Product Innovations', *European Journal of Innovation Management*, 9 (1), 20–43.

Hill T. (1987), *Manufacturing Strategy. The Strategic Management of the Manufacturing Function*, London: Macmillan.

Hitt, M.A. R.D. Ireland and R.E. Hoskisson (1997), *Strategic Management*, St Paul - Minneapolis: West Publishing Company.

Hofer C.W. and D. Schendel (1978), *Strategic Formulation: Analytical Concepts*, St Paul - Minneapolis: West Publishing Co.

Hughes W.R. (1971), 'Scale Frontiers in Electric Power', in W.M. Capron (ed.), *Technological Change in Regulated Industries*, Washington: The Brookings Institution.

Huston L. and N. Sakkab (2006), 'Connect and Develop. Inside Procter & Gamble's New Model for Innovation', *Harvard Business Review*, March, 58–66.

Iansiti M. (1993), 'Real World R&D: Jumping the Product Generation Gap', *Harvard Business Review*, May, 69–78.

Jones O. (2000), 'Innovation Management as a Post-Modern Phenomenon: the Outsourcing of Pharmaceutical R&D', *British Journal of Management*, 11, 341–356.

Kotable M. and K.S. Swan (1995), 'The Role of Strategic Alliances in High Technology New Product Development', *Strategic Management Journal*, 16, 621–636.

Kotler P. (1990), *Marketing Management*, Englewood Cliffs, NJ: Prentice Hall.

La Repubblica, Affari e Finanza (2006), 'Acciaio, Arvedi Raddoppia con l'High-tech', 18 Settembre, 12.

Lambin J.J. (1996), *Marketing Stratégique et Opérationnel*, Paris: Dunod.

Leonard-Barton D.L. (1992), 'Core Capabilities and Core Rigidities', *Strategic Management Journal*, special issue, Summer, 111–125.

Levitt T. (1963a), 'Exploit the Product Life Cycle', *Harvard Business Review*, Nov. –Dec., 81–94.

Levitt T. (1963), 'Creativity is not Enough', *Harvard Business Review*; reprinted in Best of HBR (2002), August, 137–147.

Levy H. and M. Sarnat (1986), *Capital Investment and Financial Decisions*, Englewood Cliffs: Prentice Hall.

Lieberman M. (1984), 'The Learning Curve and Pricing in the Chemical Processing Industries', *Rand Journal of Economics*, 15, Summer, 213–228.

Lieberman M., L.J. Lan and M.D. Williams (1990), 'Firm Level Productivity and Management Influence: A Comparison of U.S. and Japanese Automobile Producers', *Management Science*, 36 (10), 1193–1215.

Lorenzoni G. (ed.) (1992), *Accordi, Reti e Vantaggio Competitivo*, Milano: EtasLibri.

Macioce A. (2001), 'L'Innovazione Tecnologica nelle Medie e Piccole Imprese', in F. Fontana and P. Boccardelli (eds), *L'Innovazione Tecnologica nelle Medie e Piccole Imprese*, Roma: Luiss Edizioni.

Malerba F. (1992), 'Learning by Firms and Incremental Technical Change', *Economic Journal*, 94, 213–228.

Mariotti S. and P. Migliarese (1984), 'Organizzazione Industriale e Rapporti fra Imprese in un Settore ad Elevato Tasso Innovativo', *L'Industria*, 1, January, 71–100.

Martins E.C. and F. Terblanche (2003), 'Building Organisational Culture that Stimulates Creativity and Innovation', *European Journal of Innovation Management*, 6, 64–74.

McGahan A. (2004), 'How Industries Change', *Harvard Business Review*, Oct., 87–93.

Mediobanca R&S (1970), *L'Industria Chimica*, Milano: R&S.

Melewicki D. and H. Sivakumar (2004), 'Patents and Product Development Strategies: A Model of Antecedents and Consequences of Patent Value', *European Journal of Innovation Management*, 7 (1) 5–22.

Mintzberg H. (1983), *Structure in Five: Designing Effective Organizations*, Englewood Cliffs: Prentice Hall.

Mintzberg H. (1990), 'The Design School: Reconsidering the Basic Premises of Strategic Management', *Strategic Management Journal*, 11 (3), March–April, 171–195.

Modigliani F. (1958), 'New Developments on the Oligopoly Front', *Journal of Political Economy*, 66, June, 215–232.

Mueller D.C. (1986), *Profits in the Long Run*, Cambridge: Cambridge University Press.

Munari F. and M. Sobrero (eds) (2004), *Innovazione Tecnologica e Gestione d'Impresa*, Bologna: Il Mulino.

Nelson R. (1993), *National Innovation Systems: A Comparative Analysis*, Oxford: Oxford University Press.

Norman R. and R. Ramirez (1994), *Designing Interactive Strategy. From Value Chain to Value Constellation*, New York: John Wiley & Sons.

Paine Webber (1995), *World Steel Dynamics*, Paine Webber, New York.

Pammolli F. (1996), *Innovazione, Concorrenza e Strategie di Sviluppo nell'Industria Farmaceutica*, Milano: Guerrini Scientifica.

Pavitt K. (1984), 'Sectorial Patterns of Technical Change. Toward a Taxonomy and a Theory', *Research Policy*, 13 (6), 343–373.

Peterlaf M.A. (1993), 'The Cornerstones of Competitive Advantages: A Resource Based View', *Strategic Management Journal*, 14, 179–191.

Phillips A. (1971), *Technology and Market Structure*, Lexington: Heath-Lexington Books .

Piccaluga A. (1996), *Imprese e Sistema dell'Innovazione Tecnologica*, Milano: Guerini Scientifica.

Pisano G.P. (1990), 'The R&D Boundaries of the Firm. An Empirical Analysis', *Administrative Science Quarterly*, 34, 153–176.

Pisano G., W. Shan and D. Teece (1988), 'Joint Ventures and Collaboration in the Biotechnology Industry', in D.C. Mowery (ed.), *International Collaborative Ventures in US Manufacturing*, Cambridge: Ballinger.

Porter M.E. (1980), *Competitive Strategy*, New York: Free Press.

Porter M.E. (1985), *Competitive Advantage*, New York: Free Press.

Porter M.E. (1991), 'Towards a Dynamic Theory of Strategy', *Strategic Management Journal*, 12, 95–117.

Porter M.E. (1994), 'Towards a Dynamic Theory of Strategy', in R.P. Rumelt, D.E. Schendel and D.J. Teece (eds), *Fundamental Issues in Strategy*, Boston: Harvard Business Press.

Prahalad C.K and Gary Hamel (1990), 'The Core Competences of the Corporation', *Harvard Business Review*, May–June, 79–91.

Pratten C.F. (1971), *Economies of Scale in Manufacturing Industry*, Cambridge: Cambridge University Press.

Rappaport A. (1986), *Creating Shareholder Value. The New Standard for Business Performance*, New York: The Free Press.

Reekie W.D. (1978), 'Price and Quality Competition in the US Drug Industry', *Journal of Industrial Economics*, 26, 223–237.

Robinson and C. Lakhani (1975), 'Dynamic Price Models for New-Product Planning', *Management Science*, 10, June, 1113–1122.

Rosemberg N. (1976), 'On Technological Expectation', *The Economic Journal*, Sept.

Ross D. (1986), 'Learning to Dominate', *Journal of Industrial Economics*', 34, 337–353.

Ross S.A., R.W. Westerfield and J. Jaffe (1999), *Corporate Finance*, Boston: McGraw-Hill.

Rumelt R.P. (1986), *Strategy, Structure and Economic Performance*, Boston: Harvard Business School Press.

Rumelt R.P., D.E. Shendel and D.J. Teece (1994), *Fundamental Issues in Strategy*, Boston: Harvard Business School Press.

Russel M., P. Takac and L. Usher (2004), 'Industry Productivity Trends under the North American Industry Classification System', *Monthly Labour Review*, November, 31–42.

Russo M. (1996), *Cambiamento Tecnico e Relazioni fra Imprese. Il Distretto Ceramico di Sassuolo*, Torino: Rosemberg & Sellier.

Salter W.E.G. (1966), *Productivity and Technical Change*, Cambridge: Cambridge University Press.

Schendel D.E. and C.W. Hofer (1979), *Strategic Management: a New View of Business Policy and Planning*, Boston: Little, Brown.

Scherer R.M. and D. Ross (1990), *Industrial Market Structure and Economic Performance*, Boston: Houghton and Mifflin.

Schumpeter J. (1942), *Capitalism, Socialism and Democracy*, New York: Harper & Row.

Sen F. and A.H. Rubenstein (1989), 'External Technology and In-House R&D's Facilitative Role', *Journal of Product Innovation Management*, 6 (2), 123–138.

Sobrero M. (1999), *La Gestione dell'Innovazione: Strategie, Organizzazione e Tecniche Operative*, Roma: Carocci.

Sobrero, M. (2001), 'Innovazione Tecnologica: Competenze e Sviluppo della Piccola e Media Impresa', in F. Fontana and P. Boccardelli (eds), *L'Innovazione Tecnologica nelle Medie e Piccole Imprese*, Roma: Luiss Edizioni.

Solow R. (1960), 'Investment and Technological Change', in K. Arrow, S. Karlin and P. Supples (eds), *Mathematical Models in the Social Sciences*, Stanford: Stanford University Press.

Stalk G. and T.M. Hout (1990), *Competing Against Time*, New York: The Free Press.

Steele H. (1964), 'Patent Restrictions and Price Competition in the Ethical Drugs Industry', *The Journal of Industrial Economics*, 12 (3),198–223.

Sylos Labini P. (1964), *Oligopolio e Progresso Tecnico*, Torino: Einaudi.

Teece D.J. (ed.) (1987), *The Competitive Challenge. Strategies for Industrial Innovation and Renewal*, Cambridge, MA: Ballinger.

Teece D.J. (2007), 'Explicating Dynamic Capabilities: the Nature and Microfoundations of (Sustainable) Enterprise Performance', *Strategic Management Journal*, published online in Wiley Interscience.

Teece D.J. and G. Pisano (1994), 'The Dynamic Capabilities of Firms: An Introduction', *Industrial and Corporate Change*, 3 (3), 537–556.

Teece D.J., G. Pisano and A. Shuen (1997), 'Dynamic Capabilities and Strategic Management', *Strategic Management Journal*, 18 (7), August, 509–533.

Thompson A.A. and A.J. Strickland (1998), *Strategic Management Concepts and Cases*, Boston: McGraw Hill.

Thurow L. (1992), *Head to Head*, Cambridge, MA: MIT Press.

Tushman M.L. and P. Anderson (1986), 'Technological Discontinuities and Organizational Environments', *Administrative Science Quarterly*, 31 (3), 439–65.

United States Department of Labor (2006), 'Productivity and Cost by Industry: Manufacturing', U.S. Department of Labor, Bureau of Labor Statistics, 2 May, Washington.

Williamson J.R. (1992), 'How Sustainable is Our Competitive Advantage?', *California Management Review*, 34 (3), 29–51.

Wonglimpiyarat J. (2004), 'The Use of Strategies in Managing Technological Innovation', *European Journal of Innovation Management*, 7 (3), 229–250.

Zirger B.J. and M.A. Maidique (1990), 'A Model of New Product Development. An Empirical Test', *Management Science*, 36 (7), 867–883.

Index